UNIVERSITY ON TRIAL

UNIVERSITY ON TRIAL

The Case of the University of North Carolina

Robert A. Dentler
D. Catherine Baltzell
Daniel J. Sullivan

Abt Books

Cambridge, Massachusetts

Reissued by arrangement with
University Press of America, Inc.
4720 Boston Way
Lanham, MD 20706

Library of Congress Cataloging in Publication Data

Dentler, Robert A., 1928–
  University on trial.

  Includes index.
  1. United States. Dept. of Education. Office
for Civil Rights.   2. University of North Carolina
(System)   3. Segregation in higher education—
Law and legislation—United States. I. Baltzell,
D. Catherine.   II. Sullivan, Daniel J. (Daniel
Joseph), 1946–   . III. Title.
KF4225.D46 1983   344.73'0798   83–2709
ISBN 0–89011–588–5   347.304798

Printed in the United States of America

Table of Contents

List of Tables

Acknowledgments

We are indebted to the help of many people in the course of writing this book, a few of whom must go unnamed because of their circumstances and the controversy that raged beneath the trial reported here. None of those who helped has contributed to our mistakes, of course, and none should be assumed to share our points of view.

Helen Dentler shared in touring the campuses of the University of North Carolina, and guided the preparation of our index; hence she is a member of our team. Cristina Bodinger de Uriarte served as a critically essential and sociologically astute research assistant to the project. Clark C. Abt encouraged us to write the book and sensed the policy importance of the trial it recounts. Jose Llanes contributed a field report on one of the colleges and offered valuable insights. Three attorneys for the Office for Civil Rights—Richard Foster, William E. Michaels, and Jeffrey F. Champagne—were our guides into the world of giving expert testimony in an administrative law proceeding. Their paralegal coworker, John Wilkerson, was the vital link between Washington, D.C. and Cambridge, Massachusetts.

Susan Brighton served as project administrative assistant. Thea Moskat helped coordinate preparation of the manuscript and typed the revisions, and Kathe Phinney typed most of the first draft. Jean Layzer and Nancy Irwin Maxwell of Abt Books gave essential editorial and production assistance.

Preface

Emile Durkheim, who founded the field of the sociology of education a century ago, depicted the structure of education as a kind of dependent outcropping from the bedrock of society. We believe he was probably correct for his time, but in the years since then, that structural relationship has become complicated in at least two ways as the interdependence between social institutions has intensified and as the pace of change has quickened. Today, education has become an *arena* in which a great variety of policy issues clash fiercely and rather openly, and educators themselves take part in the struggle to influence much larger policy outcomes. The Grove of Academe in Durkheim's era has become a kind of political and economic Super Bowl. In addition, the educational decisions made in this arena have ramifications far beyond what he called the functional transmission of culture. They now virtually forecast *future* distributions of both wealth and opportunity.

This book records and interprets one of these policy clashes. It tells the story—as yet unfinished—of how fifteen of the sixteen campuses of the University of North Carolina went to trial in the federal courts over the question of who shall teach and learn what and where across the places and programs of a vast state system of higher education. The trial focuses on constitutional questions of equal treatment and of academic freedom and states' rights, and it crystallizes around Title VI of the Civil Rights Act of 1964, which prohibits racial discrimination and segregation. Still, the story is larger than that; it is the story of a struggle over the aims and content of higher learning, and we try to capture this larger dimension in our book.

Our narrative has not been crafted from a lofty distance, and while our methods of analysis are those of the social sciences, our value preferences are actively engaged on the side of equality of access and treatment as opposed to elitism and selectivity. We entered the trial of the University of North Carolina early in 1980 as independent experts in the sociology, evaluation, and economics of education, but we entered from the side of the Office for Civil Rights, whose attorneys were charged with enforcing the Civil Rights Act. We show how that tiny federal agency bobbed and weaved uncertainly in the heavy seas of presidential administrations, and we are not its agents or apologists. In the course of analyzing issues and testifying, however, we were treated like adversaries by attorneys for the University, and we behaved accordingly.

At stake in the trial was roughly $100 million a year in federal aid, grants, and contracts to the University of North Carolina. If the University were to be found unwilling to plan and act to eliminate racial segregation in its midst, it would lose its federal aid. The actual stake in the trial is larger than this, however. As the Ford Foundation Commission on the Higher Education of Minorities found in 1982, the progress made in extending college opportunities to racial/ethnic minorities from 1965 to 1975 has slowed to a standstill in America. Black student enrollments began, in fact, to decline in 1982, and this is a predictor of trends among other minorities and among low-income groups in general. What is at stake in the larger sense, then, is essentially the inclusiveness, the relative universality, of higher education in America.

Economist Thomas Sowell was also an expert witness in the trial which is our story. He was blithely optimistic about the future of educational opportunities for black students. To him, those opportunities bubble up out of the American melting pot as each ethnic group takes its place in the line of earned upward mobility. Our view is grim by contrast. We studied the history of the University of North Carolina, as Sowell did not, and came away convinced that just as it long ago fashioned a system that would preserve the racial caste structures of the 1870–1916 era, so it has been preoccupied since 1974 with closing its gates on some campuses against some groups of students.

Our book is also a record of the steps that would have to be taken in order to create a truly inclusive and equitable public university system. In order to widen our readership, we have subordinated our statistical tables to the back of the book, but our evidence shows that the steps toward genuine equalization of opportunity would have to be much larger and bolder than the ones proposed by the University of North Carolina, if they were to result in any effects.

How could we expect that bold steps toward equality would be taken in an era that has begun to look like an *eclipse* of educational development in general? Federal disinvestments in education have occupied center stage for two years now, and cutbacks in state investments are forming chorus lines in the wings. The demographic cliff where a sharp decline in eighteen- to twenty-year-olds in the total population begins has been reached, and the smaller, more vulnerable colleges of the nation have begun to disappear. Graduate studies are in decline generally, and only community colleges really continue to expand.

Our position in this book is that constitutional democracy can never be priced out of reach and that jurisprudential safeguards against this tendency are very formidable. Our other position is that the steps toward desegregation—outreach for students, the elimination of duplication in facilities and programs, and degree program consolidation—are themselves sources of improved efficiency, reduced expenditures, and increased viability for public college campuses. That some university administrators and trustees are less concerned with these gains, and more committed to the aims of prestige and preservation of the status quo, is one of the conclusions of our book.

Moralizing aside, the story we have told lacks three ingredients of the traditional southern gothic: violent action, clear-cut villainy, and fictionality. The action is essentially academic, where the consequences can do violent harm but where the dynamics are very courteous. The academic actors, moreover, are complicated and multidimensional. Only Jesse Helms qualifies, perhaps, and his actions are executed off-stage. The attorneys and witnesses for the University, moreover, have points of merit to make and they are suffused with the righteousness of their cause.

In this respect, our book begins to reach the issue of the place of higher education in a mass, post-industrial society. We advocate for an accessible, inclusive, instructionally and fiscally equalized public university, but we do so with an awareness that there are many competing visions. The University of North Carolina is *not* an exemplar of the inaccessible, exclusive, elitist, and educatively indifferent alternative. It is a vital example of a public university that hangs in the balance between competing policy extremes. How it eventually repairs or covers over its own contradictions will signify for many less worthy universities throughout the nation.

Robert A. Dentler
D. Catherine Baltzell

Cambridge, MA

Daniel J. Sullivan, Jr.

Milwaukee, WI

Foreword

University on Trial is an important book about higher education and civil rights law. It is the story of how a great public university system failed to live up to its greatest responsibility—that of providing equal access for all to all of its publicly-supported educational units. The black struggle, these authors assert, is profoundly identified with securing educational opportunities. In North Carolina, a state with a relatively liberal reputation in race relations, blacks found the higher education opportunity system blocked, and deliberately so.

This is an important story about public policy and educational equity because it analyzes the actions of people who knew what was right but failed to do what was right. In holding up to public scrutiny the failings of a great state university system such as that in North Carolina, Robert Dentler, Catherine Baltzell, and Daniel Sullivan are going against the grain. The song that Johnnie Mercer sang years ago sums up American public opinion that one should accentuate the positive, eliminate the negative, but not mess with the "in between." North Carolina is "in between" northern and southern traditions, liberal and reactionary positions. The nation is where North Carolina is; thus an analysis of its foibles is in fact an analysis of the American condition—the American dilemma.

The activities "in between" that affect most of us remain more or less invisible because of the electronic and print media's penchant for portraying extremes—the vicious and their victims. The governor of North Carolina was like the governor of most states; he would never stand in the doorway of the university, symbolically to prohibit the entrance of black students. North Carolina would not tolerate the assembly of a howling mob of whites bent on keeping blacks from matriculating in its predominantly white colleges and universities. It is a factual statement that North Carolina facilitated impressive curricular strides by its public black colleges (although they were outpaced by their white counterparts; no black school had been elevated to the rank of a doctoral-degree granting institution). White educational administrators of the university system were annoyed that their state which had done much to foster the education of blacks remained a target of criticism and was expected to do more.

In the court case, a law firm whose partners had achieved eminence as civil rights advocates was retained as attorneys of record for the University of North Carolina system. The attorneys and their client attempted to turn the trial that alleged violation of the civil rights of blacks into one that alleged violation of the academic rights of an institution to govern itself and to deploy its resources in ways to maximize educational outcome. In the opinion of Dentler, Baltzell and Sullivan, the University of North Carolina attempted to shift the focus of concern from equal access to educational resources to that of equal provision of educational services.

Even if the University of North Carolina system had been tried on its own terms—those of providing equal educational services to its different racial populations—it would have been found wanting, according to the authors of *University on Trial*. The physical plants of most of its predominantly black colleges were inadequate, deficient, or obsolete, compared with that of most predominantly white colleges; minority administrators were few in the higher echelons of the system's bureaucracy where planning and policy decisions are made.

With a change in administration in the federal government, the parties to the court case began private negotiations, arrived at a consensus which the court decreed that terminated the trial in progress. Unable to present his analysis of the segregative actions of the University of North Carolina system in open court, Robert Dentler, an expert witness, completes the prosecution of the case in this book. If the tone is indicting, it is because the materials were gathered largely for an adversarial proceeding.

This book is devoted to an analysis of racial injustice as it has been built into the higher education system of a relatively liberal state. Reviewing the history of the issue, the authors concluded that the University of North Carolina fashioned a higher education system that would preserve the racial caste system by limiting the opportunities available to blacks. This also was the conclusion of Judge Pratt who found the University of North Carolina system racially segregated with no plans as late as 1977 to correct this violation.

Because of its location and orientation, truly one could say "as North Carolina goes, so goes the nation." It reflects our culture and its civil rights dilemma in higher education. Because of this, the analysis has implications for situations and settings beyond the state that is the subject of this study.

University on Trial explores the universal aspects of higher education that involve and go beyond racial segregation. The authors claim that what really irritated the officers of the University of North Carolina system was the challenge that the court case presented to their *vision* of higher education. They maintained it as a system that decreased matriculation opportunities for minority racial populations as the quality of educational resources increased. As evidence, a trend-line of changing proportions from high to low of blacks was seen, respectively, in schools that granted associated arts, baccalaureate, master of arts or master of science, and doctorate degrees. The racial segregation by varying levels of higher education, according to Dentler, Baltzell, and Sullivan, indicated both implicit and explicit values of the system—that racial equity can not be put above academic self-determination in the pursuit of excellence.

Values that promote and support an elite hierarchy of colleges and universities that gain prestige and esteem by denying admission and employment to a disproportionate number of racial minority students and faculty at higher levels of the hierarchy are unworthy of a public educational system, in the opinion of the authors of this book. It is well that they introduced this theme because elitism can function to exclude in an arbitrary and capricious way and thus become a form of institutional oppression as harmful as racism or sexism. The authors make a contribution to the literature of social oppression by introducing this theme in their analysis. Although elitism may not violate civil rights law, it is contrary to the customs of an open society that believes in equal opportunity and equal access. Elitism is portrayed as the stumbling block for libertarians who are against other forms of discrimination.

The focus on North Carolina in this policy study is an antidote to any unexamined belief in progress as a natural and inevitable phenomenon. The authors show that a state that has implemented good actions in some areas is capable of undertaking bad actions in others. While North Carolina, for example, has moved to increase the number of black students on predominantly white college campuses, it has taken little action to increase the number of white students on predominantly black college campuses; the State has achieved a reasonable level of integration in the faculty of its predominantly black institutions of higher education, but has done very little to desegregate the teaching faculty in predominantly white schools. Dentler, Baltzell and Sullivan describe the North Carolina higher education system as hanging in the balance between competing visions.

The significance of this book is precisely in its description of the competing visions of a state that hangs in the balance. The direction in which it is tending is an important sign. Reviewing the work of Gordon Allport and others, Thomas Pettigrew, a social psychologist, reminds us that about one-fifth of the white population in this nation is prejudiced in a reactionary way and can be counted on to oppose minorities in any circumstance. Also, about one-fifth is unprejudiced—the so-called knee-jerk liberal—and is absolutely accepting of racial minorities in an unconditional way. This leaves about three-fifths of the white population—the majority—as conformists who hang in the balance and can be swayed either way. They will go with the prevailing public opinions. They will join with advocates of the *status quo* and the rejection of racial minorities, if they are convinced it is in their interest to do so. And they will join with advocates of social change and the acceptance of racial minorities, if they are convinced it is in their interest to do so. *University on Trial* examines this phenomenon and provides insight regarding the direction in which the nation is tending. A future intolerant of racism could embrace elitism and its irrational justifications for rejection, according to the story that unfolds in this book. Thus, there is little cause for celebration in the progress of a nation that advocates elitism. It, too, is as much a form of institutional oppression as racism and sexism. In the North Carolina case, a higher education system was on trial as well as the values that support and sustain it. Although the trial was aborted, this nation eventually must render a verdict.

Charles V. Willie
Harvard University

CHAPTER 1

The Dispute in Context

The Supreme Court's 1954 declaration, in *Brown v. Board of Education of Topeka*,[1] that officially maintained racial segregation was unconstitutional, laid to rest an issue as old as the founding of the republic: the issue of how black children and youth should be treated by the state. *Brown* made the connection between racial fairness and educational equity direct and unequivocal.

Brown stated that segregation was legally wrong because it denied blacks the coequal status due all Americans, and *Brown* defined segregation as an indicator of the persisting vestiges of slavery and the caste system that slavery spawned. Fifteen years after Gunnar Myrdal had characterized the "American dilemma" as the continuing disparity between the vision of equal treatment for all citizens and the unequal treatment of black Americans,[2] *Brown* moved with the force of law to resolve the disparity. It did so by linking racial fairness, equal treatment, and equal educational opportunity, and by specifying that the cycle of inequality could be broken by abolishing state-imposed racial separation. *Brown* supposed that when such separation was abolished, racially *dual* systems of education would wither away or be eliminated by court action and that black students would then be free to succeed or fail on the basis of merit rather than caste.

The *Brown* decision was by no means limited to public elementary and secondary schools; it applied to all levels of schooling created and maintained by the state, from infant development centers to postdoctoral programs. Other court decisions and legislation fol-

1

lowed quickly in its wake, extending the central principle of racial justice to many other spheres of public service, from transportation to medical care.

In fact, the major legal precedents for *Brown* came from decisions bearing on public colleges and universities. Class actions as well as individual suits grew up in the 1930s and 1940s under initiatives taken against segregated universities. In *Missouri ex. rel. Gaines v. Canada* (1938), the first major victory for the National Association for the Advancement of Colored People (NAACP) in a series of such efforts, the Supreme Court decided that if states failed to provide college facilities for blacks equal to those provided for whites, then they had to admit blacks to previously white-only campuses.[3] *Sweatt v. Painter*[4] and *McLaurin v. Oklahoma State Regents*[5] advanced the principle even further, years before *Brown*.

In the years just after the *Brown* decision in 1954, most states repealed their laws designed to preserve racially segregated public colleges and universities. Others held fast to custom, however, and in 1962 James Meredith's court-ordered admission to that bastion of white supremacy, the University of Mississippi, triggered a violent conflict on the day of his arrival. In the same year, Governor George Wallace tried in person to prevent the enrollment of Autherine Lucey at the University of Alabama, where a riot ensued.

After these test cases, racial segregation in public higher education began to *seem* to be indefensible, politically as well as legally. The nineteen states that had maintained minority segregated public colleges for anywhere from fifty to one hundred years changed their laws early in the 1960s, and as the number of black students enrolled in colleges doubled during that decade, the public gained the impression that the walls of racial segregation had crumbled.

Still, those nineteen states today maintain thirty-four predominantly black public colleges and universities. These campuses enrolled nearly 145,000 students in 1977, more than 90 percent of them black, and these students comprise one-fourth of all black students enrolled in four-year colleges in the nation. What is more, as recently as 1970, all but a tiny handful of these thirty-four colleges had comparatively underqualified and underpaid faculties, deficient plants, and poor equipment and materials, and they hosted economically impoverished students who had been poorly prepared for college.[6]

The Civil Rights Act of 1964 created the Office for Civil Rights (OCR) within the Department of Health, Education and Welfare (HEW). Among other duties, OCR was charged with monitoring and enforcing parts of the Act, including Title VI, which says: "No person in the United States shall, on the grounds of race, color, or national origin, be excluded from participation in, be denied the benefits of, or be subjected to discrimination under any program or activity receiving federal financial assistance." By that time, state university systems were receiving from $20 million to $100 million a year in federal assistance, so they were certainly captured in the regulatory net of Title VI.

In 1968, at the tag end of the Johnson Administration, OCR completed an analysis of evidence on state colleges and announced that it had found *ten* states that were continuing to operate segregated campuses in violation of Title VI. OCR directed Arkansas, Florida, Georgia, Louisiana, Maryland, Mississippi, North Carolina, Oklahoma, Pennsylvania, and Virginia to prepare and submit corrective plans.

THE ADAMS CASE

As the Nixon Administration took over in 1969, it became apparent that enforcement of Title VI was going to have a very low priority. Some states, including North Carolina, ignored the directive, and others filed vague memoranda of intentions. The Legal Defense Fund (LDF) of the NAACP and the law firm of Rauh, Silard and Lichtman therefore filed suit in October 1970 on behalf of Adams, a black Mississippian and father of six children, who complained that his rights and those of his children under Title VI were being violated. More crucially, perhaps, Adams sued senior HEW officials, including Secretary Elliot Richardson, alleging defaults in their execution of Title VI responsibilities.

U.S. District Court Judge John Pratt agreed with Adams.[7] He found HEW's policy to be one of "benign neglect." In *Adams v. Richardson*, Judge Pratt concluded that HEW "had not properly fulfilled its obligation under Title VI . . . to eliminate the vestiges of past policies and practices of segregation in programs receiving federal financial assistance." He ordered HEW to begin compliance proceedings within four months against the states that had not submitted acceptable plans.

Adams became a landmark case in both education and civil rights law: it spanned ten states, it decided that those states maintained segregative colleges, it found the federal government liable for failure to obey the Civil Rights Act, and it required a speedy remedy. It also took cognizance of the finding of the U.S. Commission on Civil Rights that southern states had, by 1964, done almost nothing about complying with *Brown* in their colleges. In that year, traditionally white institutions in the University of North Carolina system, for example, remained 99 percent white, and the traditionally black institutions remained 99.9 percent black. In 1969, five years after the Civil Rights Act, the white campuses had moved by one percentage point to become 98 percent white.

The *Adams* liability opinion was so grave that HEW appealed it almost immediately. The U.S. Court of Appeals for the District of Columbia decided to hear the appeal *en banc*—that is, with all eleven judges attending—because of the exceptional importance of the issues involved. That court unanimously affirmed Judge Pratt's opinion, although it gave HEW 180 additional days in which to act.[8]

HEW then asked the ten states, once again, to file plans. Eight states, including North Carolina, complied. Louisiana and Mississippi were referred to the Department of Justice for what were supposed to be immediate enforcement proceedings for noncompliance. HEW announced in 1974 that the other eight states had all filed acceptable plans.

LDF attorneys and Joseph Rauh of Rauh, Silard and Lichtman studied the new state plans, however, and found them to be very deficient. They returned to Judge Pratt's courtroom in 1975 to contest the acceptability of the plans, and in 1977 Judge Pratt ruled in *Adams v. Califano* that the plans filed by North Carolina and five of the other states "did not meet important desegregation requirements."[9] He also noted that these states had not made "significant progress toward higher education desegregation" between 1974 and 1977.

This time, Judge Pratt moved to prevent further stalling by the states or HEW. He not only directed HEW to notify the states of their noncompliance with Title VI, but he also ordered it to devise "final criteria" specifying the ingredients of an acceptable plan, for the Appeals Court had earlier noted the incompleteness of HEW's criteria. Pratt ordered that the criteria should cover matters of student admission, recruitment, and retention, the placement and duplication of degree programs across campuses, ways to enhance black colleges, and standards for changing the racial composition of faculties. By 1978, HEW had issued "Revised Criteria" and filed them with the court.

A year later, HEW reported that five of the six states covered in *Adams v. Califano* had complied, but that the University of North Carolina (UNC) had offered a plan that "offered no realistic promise of desegregating the UNC."[10] UNC had been chosen by LDF and Rauh as the main target of their legal campaign in 1974, and now it was becoming apparent why. Policymakers in North Carolina had decided in 1974 that their remedial plan had gone far enough; not only would the UNC Board of Governors go no further, but it also decided, as the pressure from HEW intensified year by year, that the federal intrusion into state affairs and into academic matters had simply gone too far.

When HEW took the first tentative steps in 1979 toward a hearing on why UNC's federal funds should not be cut off, UNC President William Friday and the Board made a critical decision. They agreed to retain Charles Morgan and his senior associate, Joseph J. Levin, as legal counsel to fight the impending, presumably fateful, dispute. Roughly $100 million a year in federal support was at stake. Without it, UNC could suffer nearly fatal damage to many of its most prestigious programs. Morgan was one of the nation's more famous civil rights and civil liberties trial lawyers. A graduate of the University of Alabama, Morgan had assisted Autherine Lucey, Martin Luther King, Jr., and countless other Deep South civil rights activists, working in Birmingham and Atlanta from 1963 until 1973, when he relocated in Washington, D.C. Joseph Levin had directed the Southern Poverty Law Center from its inception in Atlanta, Georgia.

These resilient, ingenious attorneys quickly went on the offensive. They filed suit, not in Washington, D.C., where Judge Pratt presided, but in the Eastern District of North Carolina, in Raleigh, to block the HEW proceeding and to prevent enforcement of the Revised Criteria. Judge Franklin T. Dupree of Raleigh refused HEW's request to remove the case to Judge Pratt, but he also denied UNC's requests and called instead for a formal hearing before an administrative law judge in Washington.

That hearing began in July 1980. Before it was two months old, the presiding Judge, Lewis F. Parker, excused himself from the case, explaining that his daughter had just applied for admission to UNC at Chapel Hill. He was replaced by Judge John Mathias, and with that the hearing got underway in earnest, building in one year to nearly 15,000 pages of testimony and over 500 exhibits.

By 1981, HEW had become two federal departments. Secretary Califano had departed and Shirley Hufstedler had become the Secretary of the new Department of Education. Califano and OCR had acted in 1979, however, to prepare for the UNC case by recruiting Richard Foster, an experienced trial lawyer, from the Georgetown University law faculty, and by teaming him with two veterans of OCR Title VI battles, William Michaels and Jeffrey Champagne.

Months before the hearing began, it became obvious that Morgan and Levin intended to make the hearing as much of a retrial of the substance of *Adams* as they possibly could. They were not going to litigate on the narrow issue of whether UNC was in violation of the

OCR request for an acceptable remedial plan. Instead, they sought and got preliminary approval of their definition of the issues to be heard, usually using the due process principle for leverage in their arguments. As a result, the issues were framed between November 1979 and June 1980 as these: the history of OCR-UNC relations, 1965–1980; the nature of racial segregation in higher education; evidence of segregative acts and outcomes; states' rights; university governance and academic freedom; the Revised Criteria for Desegregating; and so forth.

As Morgan and Levin prepared to spend millions of dollars in developing an all-embracing defense of UNC policies and practices, Foster, Michaels, and Champagne got authorization to reach far beyond OCR for assistance. They contracted with the accounting firm of Price, Waterhouse to collect and verify data on the financial records of UNC. They also contracted with DBS Inc., a data processing and analysis firm in nearby Virginia with long experience in handling statistics related to educational and civil rights, to collect, tabulate, and graph some twenty-three volumes of data on UNC's staff, courses, degree programs, and enrollments.

Foster also invited eight experts on higher education to testify, including Harold Howe, then Vice President of the Ford Foundation, Charles V. Willie, Professor at Harvard University, and Robert A. Dentler, Senior Sociologist at Abt Associates Inc. Later, Foster enlarged his request to Dentler, and OCR contracted with Abt Associates to establish a study project team composed of Dentler, D. Catherine Baltzell, Daniel J. Sullivan, and Cristina Bodinger-de Uriarte, to analyse and interpret many portions of the mass of evidence.

While the hearing was in progress, Ronald Reagan was elected President. The appointive officers of the Department of Education and OCR turned over. Within about a month after the inauguration of Reagan, United States Senator Jesse Helms of North Carolina managed to enlist Education Secretary Terrell Bell and others in the start-up of secret consent decree negotiations between UNC officers and attorneys and OCR officers, a special counsel for Bell, and Foster.[11] Between March and June of 1981, then, the government settled its dispute with UNC. The proposed settlement was put before Judge Dupree in Raleigh on June 22.

The LDF and Rauh promptly tried to restrain Secretary Bell from entering into the consent decree, but Judge Pratt said he lacked jurisdiction and Judge Dupree denied their motion. They then filed an appeal with the District of Columbia circuit. A three-judge panel heard arguments on January 8, 1982, and decided in August 1982 that the consent decree ratified by Judge Dupree in Raleigh, as well as the propriety of its development, were moot issues for their circuit.

On a 2–1 vote, the majority noted that "the day has not yet come when courts of one circuit should issue declaratory judgments evaluating actions taken by courts of another circuit." Joseph Levin's device of consolidating jurisdiction under Judge Dupree in North Carolina *appeared*, one year after Dupree's acceptance of the settlement, to have triumphed.

Appeals Court Judge Skelly Wright dissented very strongly, however. In an opinion some five times the length of the majority report, Wright reconsidered the whole history of the case. As we examine his dissent in Chapter Five of this book, we will here remark only that the dissent contains a very strong challenge to the legal soundness of the majority opinion and to the correctness of Judge Pratt's finding: "Despite commendable diligence over the years in assuring that the Department (HEW) fulfilled its legal obligations, the District Judge suddenly rules that he lacked jurisdiction."[12] Wright ends by using Pratt's own term, "a policy of benign neglect," aiming this at the Department of Education, yet also linking it to Pratt's action.

In October 1982, the Court of Appeals stunned many observers by announcing that it will *rehear* the appeal, *en banc*. Once again, all eleven judges will gather to consider a grave question generated from the *Adams* case. The consent decree is again at risk. Responsibility has extended to include the Court of Appeals itself, two district courts, and perhaps Senator Helms, as well as the original parties and intervenors. UNC's $100 million-a-year stake in the case has been renewed.

BLACK AMERICANS IN HIGHER EDUCATION

Most of the rest of this book will be devoted to racial injustice as it has become built into the UNC system. In order to treat that subject understandably, however, we must provide more background on how things got to where they are today in American public higher education as a whole.

A Historical Overview

The periods of development in higher education for black Americans may be summarized in this way:

- First Era, 1636–1865: No opportunity for access or study, except at four schools formed between 1850 and 1865.

- Second Era, 1866–1915: Growth of a network of forty black institutions, *de jure* segregated, poor, but influential in building a base for mass literacy.

- Third Era, 1916–1930: Blacks enter white graduate and professional schools, and some whites enroll in black colleges, but segregation also hardens.

- Fourth Era, 1931–1954: Rising tide of civil rights litigation opens access for blacks to white universities.

- Fifth Era, 1955–1973: *De jure* segregation ended, Civil Rights Act, *Adams* decision, great expansion of college attendance among black Americans.

The quest for racial justice in higher education began after the Civil War. At that time, fewer than 5 percent of the nation's black population of 4.5 million could read or write.[13] Lincoln University and Wilberforce College were the only two colleges created for blacks and by black leaders (with support from white abolitionists) before 1865. Fisk University and Talledega College followed in that year.

Between 1866 and the "separate but equal" decision of *Plessy* in 1896,[14] affirming segregation, some seventeen more public colleges for blacks were formed, most of them growing up out of high schools to become normal schools to prepare black teachers and nurses. It was in the 1866–1916 period that most black colleges developed distinctive campuses and programs resting carefully on the premise of a racial caste system in the larger society. This was the same period when the Land Grant College Act, or Morrill Act, was revised in order to provide federal aid to build and operate separate black land grant colleges. None offered a liberal arts and science degree before 1916, and most were two-year technical and agricultural schools. Funding from all sources was intentionally unequal, on the assumption that blacks needed less advanced learning than whites and that lower-level instruction ought to cost less.[15]

The caste system was bruised but not broken by the impact of World War I, and in the Third Era (1916–1930) the black campuses matured while new, sometimes more rigorous academic standards were introduced. The pride of black alumni in the educative power of black colleges intensified, and the benefits from their services expanded to touch all strata. Illiteracy among blacks plummeted from 60 percent in 1895 to 25 percent in 1930.[16] Degree programs multiplied into nearly all fields, and graduates went on to graduate school and professional attainment at white universities. Segregation under state law was preserved, but World War I brought hundreds of thousands of blacks into the North, and new educational opportunities there began to be used.

The years from the Great Depression until *Brown* (the Fourth Era) laid the foundation for the patterns characteristic of the 1980s. Some black colleges developed comparatively strong academic reputations and began to produce networks of professional, commercial, and political leaders. Fisk University, Hampton Institute, Lincoln University, Howard University, Morehouse College, and Spellman College were in this league. Howard University and North Carolina Agricultural and Technical State University became generators of civil rights and other forms of radical political activism among some faculty and students. And, as we noted earlier, lawsuit after lawsuit was launched by black leaders and white allies against the white campus bastions of white separatism, the state universities from the Carolinas to Texas and Oklahoma. For all this evolution, however, most public black campuses remained cut off from opportunity, captured within and without by the persisting forces of the caste system.

It was in the 1931–1954 period that the black undergraduate colleges consolidated their mission as massive providers of opportunity. Some 96 percent of all black college students in the South were enrolled in these black colleges, and a kind of "double design" had taken form. Litigation and other civil rights pressures were opening the doors of white institutions, and blacks were entering northern white universities; at the same time, the mission of the black colleges had become a permanent part of the collegiate landscape, with sacrifices too deep and investments in them far too gigantic to allow them to falter, let alone be dissolved. Hence, in the 1960s, scholars and policy analysts began to reappraise the nature and worth of the black campuses.[17] This, in turn, was reinforced by the renewed emergence of black pride. One educator said in eulogizing Martin Luther King, Jr. that he never could have been who he became if he had gone to Harvard College. His undergraduate years at Morehouse College, a traditionally black school, were his formative ones.

A fifth era extended from *Brown* to *Adams,* and the magnitude of its impact has yet to be comprehended within higher education circles. As the 1960s took shape, the contrast between the civil rights revolution and the countercultural explosion blurred for a time, as youth leaders took their organizing tactics and action techniques from the civil rightists. By the close of the decade, however, the differences clarified and it became obvious that the black struggle was genuinely identified with securing higher educational opportunities, the historic aim; countercultural groups, on the other hand, spanned a great diversity of interests, some of them a diversion from racial justice. To this extent, black civil rightists again exerted a stabilizing influence on higher education by taking its mission seriously.

We are now in a Sixth Era. It entails a swinging back, a reversal of the expansionary, optimistic, equalizing trends of the 1955–1973 era. It also entails the confrontation of increasingly refined policy issues, some of which do not yield at all easily to the broad claims of correcting racial injustices. For example, the cruelest dragon of educational deprivation, state-imposed segregation, has been slain. There is not a single public college in the land that is now closed by law to any racial group.

When the Internal Revenue Service (IRS) acted in January 1982 to scrap the rule against tax exemptions for racially discriminatory schools and colleges, it issued a long list of so-called Christian academies in grades one through twelve, but it announced that *only* Bob Jones University of South Carolina, among the nation's 2500 colleges and universities, still subscribed to racial discrimination. We doubt that the IRS, which waived the rule after twelve years of enforcement, is a reliable source to cite, but its statement does mean that discrimination of the explicit, law-based sort has all but disappeared from the American college scene. Even Bob Jones University has admitted black students—and then has prevented them from interracial "dating" (defined to include walking together across campus for other than classroom or study purposes!) and marriage.

As a result of this reduction in law-based discrimination, access to college by blacks has multiplied steadily. Since 1970 the traditionally white state universities from coast to coast have begun to host rising numbers of blacks and other minority students.[18] This has created a widespread public impression that equity has been attained in higher education. Simultaneously, some historically black colleges have hosted more nonblack students and have created a rationale for their continuation as uniquely valuable institutions.

With the expansion of relatively inexpensive and inclusive opportunities in colleges, the notion that racial injustice remains began to seem irritating to members of a number of interest groups ranging from faculty to white alumni. The reactions are symbolized by the *Bakke v. Regents of the University of California* decision,[19] which applied the brakes to some of the wheels driving affirmative action in student admissions. By 1978 a coalition of university officers and boards began to protest the paperwork burdens and other intrusions of federal agencies charged with inspecting and enforcing civil rights regulations.

In these and other ways, then, the broad base of support for the work of LDF narrowed severely in the aftermath of *Adams*. A new kind of taboo against dealing openly with racial equity began to develop in higher education in the 1970s—not a taboo against the gains already made in the 1954–1973 period, but a pervasive avoidance of the question of what remains to be done. The same taboo carries with it the strong sense that the policy changes implicit in the laws and court decisions are indeed underway and will carry themselves along under the "natural" institutional impetus of campus-level self-reform.

Jack Greenberg of LDF, Joseph Rauh, and those who carried the action through *Adams* are not convinced of the integrity of this process, for reasons explored in every chapter of this book. These trial lawyers by 1975 were working in relative isolation, however. As black college leaders came to see it by 1975, desegregation then pointed at the still segregated black colleges in a way that seemed to threaten their survival. The final paradox of the civil rights movement seems foreshadowed in the warnings of black college presidents that their campuses would "slowly fade to white," and that if this happened, their "special mission" would fade as well.[20] Some of them fear that if they lose their racial distinctiveness, they will also be plunged into a losing race for state resources, faculty, and students, and that as the college-aged population dwindles and retrenchment sets in after 1982, a desegregation strategy could prove fatal.

The Special Role of Traditionally Black Institutions

To the extent the special mission of black colleges grew up out of the 1896–1954 conditions of legislated segregation, a racial caste system in the Deep South, and an extreme absence of equal opportunities for most blacks, that unique mission is obsolete today. Black college leaders believe, however, that because of their unique historical experience, their faculties and programs are better suited to providing effective learning opportunities for a wider range of ability levels than are white colleges. They have not explained how "fading to white" would erode that effectiveness; perhaps in achieving sameness, their specialness would be sacrificed to other objectives.

At least six black state college campuses have been desegregated since *Adams:* Bluefield State College in West Virginia, West Virginia State College, Tennessee State University, Bowie State College in Maryland, Delaware State College, and Lincoln University in Missouri. Desegregation of two others is in progress. Among these schools, only Bluefield saw its black enrollment drop dramatically— from 95 percent to 13 percent—and this is because the college became a nonresidential campus, serving commuters in a region that is 95 percent white. None has lost viability, and most are enjoying improvements in state funding.

Colleges and universities of all kinds are relatively unique institutions with a culture, organizational structure, and an input-output process of consequence for students. And, part of their uniqueness results from the *autonomy* of function accorded them, which is greater than that enjoyed by many other social institutions. For these reasons, our background for the analysis must paint in some features of black and white state colleges and universities.

All but a very few of the black colleges had been established between 1880 and 1920 as normal schools to prepare teachers for segregated black schools and to upgrade the employability of blacks in some sectors of agriculture, industry, and such human service occupations as nursing and social work. The fit between their course offerings and the notions common to the era of Booker T. Washington concerning the practical fields suitable for service in a caste-based society was very close.

Important changes took place in their offerings in the period from *Brown* to 1969. College enrollment of blacks doubled between 1960 and 1970, and though much of this tremendous expansion went into community colleges on the one hand and predominantly white universities on the other, many public black colleges did make impressive strides in curriculum, plant improvements, and faculty-building across that decade. Yet, as they improved and expanded, they were also outpaced by their counterparts. In some instances, new white campuses were created and some old ones were built up deliberately during this decade in order to avoid desegregation.

Much of the literature about black colleges in the 1960s concentrated on questions of appraising their limitations. The stress was so marked that it was not until the *Adams* controversy dragged on through the 1970s that the special merits of these campuses—apart from the handful of top-flight private schools—came to be at all widely understood.[21] For example, these colleges, public as well as private, clung to some nineteenth-century ideals of ethical development, values education, leadership preparation, health concerns, and civic responsibility long after references to these virtues had been expunged from their white counterparts.

The black colleges (we will call them TBIs, for traditionally black institutions) were also distinctive in their view of *open enrollment*. Long after the TWIs (our shorthand for the traditionally white institutions) had moved toward more or less emphatic selective standards, thereby placing themselves in the stratification schema shared by most graduate universities, the TBIs welcomed students at all levels of preparation and with a wide range of scores on test-based measures of ability and then tailored instruction to meet their diverse abilities.[22] The TBIs also preserved from their unique origins their explicit commitments to *practical community service* and problem-solving. Community service aims often included evening extension and part-time programs for mature, working people.

None of these themes in the period from 1960 to 1970 would concern us if they were not in such marked contrast to trends in higher education generally in the same period. There, the clues to church-relatedness were disappearing at all save private Roman Catholic and fundamentalist TWIs. *In loco parentis* policies were being swept away on a tide of student objections, and with them went required courses in health and hygiene, physical education, and anything about preparation for citizenship.

More crucial, perhaps, is the contrast with respect to instructional mission. At the TWIs, the B.A. and the B.S. were becoming preparatory programs for graduate and professional study or for business training inside the corporations. And, 1960 to 1970 was the era of the multiversity, of great expansion in graduate studies, and of the decay of policies about core curricula and distributive course requirements. It was also a time of heavy transfer movement by white students from campus to campus, and a time of inattention to undergraduate teaching among faculty who were eager to do research, to consult, and to build prestigious graduate programs.

Flagship campuses, so-called, from Chapel Hill to Ann Arbor to Eugene, Oregon, were busy consolidating their reputations as graduate centers, while new "branch campuses" were being built everywhere. The State University of New York at Buffalo, for instance, planned a campus to host 35,000 students but by 1979 enrollment had not exceeded 15,000. The branch campuses were often stratified, as in Pennsylvania, where Penn State remained very selective while less able students were channeled into the other campuses. As expansion and specialization by locality evolved at a furious pace, moreover, the concept of increasingly centralized *state systems* took root. State university administrative headquarters doubled their staffs, built new headquarters buildings, and intensified their planning and program review operations.

Black colleges remained at the periphery of these trends, which passed through public higher education without modifying them much. They were often routinely incorporated into the unifying state systems, and their budgets rose, but they were in many other ways left unaffected and ignored. In 1978, for example, U.S. District Judge Frank Johnson found that Alabama State University (a TBI) was guilty of discriminating against whites. At the time that suit began, *all* faculty and administrators were black. More indicatively, Judge Johnson wrote that the president of the institution "runs A.S.U. like an administrative tyrant."[23] Not mentioned was the fact that nearly all TBI chancellors and presidents were appointed by overwhelmingly *white* state system officers, state boards, and governors. The black officers could hardly be expected to be selected as advocates of rapid change in any aspect of the *status quo ante*, from desegregation to competing for research resources, in systems in which they were separate caretakers of a special population. Some commentators on Judge Johnson's opinion also overlooked the fact that A.S.U. had been pitted historically against a TWI, Auburn University, which purchased a handsome extension campus in 1967 in Montgomery, the site of A.S.U. When A.S.U. attempted through litigation to prevent this duplication, its effort was rejected.

Few studies of the TBIs in the 1955–1973 period compared them with equivalent TWIs in the public sector. Later research qualified and particularized the picture of the TBIs as uniformly deficient in faculty and quality of instruction relative to their TWI counterparts.[24] In short, there are some respects in which the TWIs and TBIs are similar, most of them looking more like replicable models of American academia than like anything else. What is more, most of the thirty-four TBIs have a far better racial and ethnic mix of faculty than their counterparts and many are better prepared to teach average to lower-ability students, a group that was expanding enormously at the TWIs everywhere by 1970.

The deep differences were racial and reputational. The TBIs neither attracted nor held many white students. Their programs of study suffered from lack of academic prestige as defined by faculty members everywhere. There were other differences, as we shall demonstrate; but in higher education, these two factors tend to determine a school's fate. It is reputation based on who enrolls and who teaches, rather than on administration, plant, programs, or actual design and delivery of instruction, that comes to determine funding, growth or decline, and many forms of extra-campus support or neglect.

What professors and (to a far lesser extent) students *think* represents quality in higher education thus has a tendency to be fulfilled over time. That thinking was, in earlier periods of American history, far more amorphous than it became during the 1960s. The SAT, for example, once limited in use to the Ivy League and a hundred other highly selective colleges, became an increasingly commonplace if specious indicator of aggregated campus "quality." Graduate centers came to be ranked by prestige according to research funding, prizes, and impact on the career marketplace. At the same time, going to college itself became less a life choice and more a perceived necessity, so that campus selection became the crux of competition among students.

In these ways, higher education itself was completing a transformation begun during World War II. It was becoming a routine part of a kindergarten-through-grade-16 system serving nearly half of the entire young adult population. Within this system, professors were working hard to protect and improve their rankings on academic selectivity.

The likelihood that professors across the nineteen states with public TBIs would include a single TBI in their precious subsystem of elite campuses was slight. Some 98 percent of those professors were white. They had not attended TBIs; indeed, in their formative years, they knew little about those campuses except that they were TBIs. Few of their graduate and professional students came from them, again a self-perpetuating pattern. Until *Brown,* and in many instances until 1964, even varsity athletic contests between TWIs and TBIs were allowed only on informal occasions. A century of racial isolation proved insurmountable so far as important changes in recognition and reputation were concerned.

However, as we will show in careful detail, the meaning of racial segregation for the black public four-year colleges of UNC, like that at very similar colleges across many states, is not limited to inferior academic reputation, nor is it merely a matter of being doomed to lag forever behind rates of expansion and improvement of the white institutions. Racial segregation is, instead, a hydra-headed monster that has stalked *all* of the campuses in states like North Carolina, where its lease on life was legally sanctioned for nearly a century. Every building, program, staff position, and network of alumni is predicated upon remnants of the racial caste system that once extended across all parts of life, but which has been breached and then broken apart in a hundred places since *Brown:* hence the anomoly of college life designed to prepare graduates for a society no longer predicated on caste. Conversely, traditionally white campuses miseducate and underprepare their graduates for this changed society.

THE CASE OF NORTH CAROLINA

North Carolina is the ideal case for the analysis of racial policies in American higher education. Unlike most other states, North Carolina embodies cultural, political, and educational characteristics that stand at a kind of explanatory midpoint between the Deep South and the North. It never built a plantation slave economy. It never generated a ruling power elite based on the plantation or, later, on industrial development. Its political commitment to some features of progressivism reaches as far back as the first writing of the U.S. Constitution, when North Carolina insisted on a Bill of Rights. Some of its Appalachian counties resisted the Confederacy and built a Republican tradition.

North Carolina was one of the first states in the South to provide for free public education for all citizens. Chapel Hill, segregated white until *Brown,* became widely known not only as a great public university but as a source of many progressive policy ideals.

Unlike other southern states, North Carolina created not one or two TBIs, but *five* in the years from 1870 to 1915. A sixth, Pembroke State, actually began as a county normal school to prepare Lumbee Indians as teachers in local Indian schools, and its unique development expresses a long history of concern in North Carolina for public educational opportunity.

The cosmopolitan, racially and educationally progressive side of North Carolina culture is best expressed in the career of Frank Porter Graham, President of the University of North Carolina from 1930 to 1949. He eliminated the "Jewish quota" policy of the medical school in a time when such quotas were used nationwide. He made Chapel Hill into a center for self-examination by the South using the tools of social science during the Great Depression, and he served on the first federal Civil Rights Commission.

North Carolina is also the state where Frank Porter Graham was defeated for reelection to the Senate by Willis Smith, who won by appealing to white racism. Smith's campaign manager was Jesse Helms, who became his assistant in Washington. Years later it was Senator Helms who in 1981 proposed legislation to cut the $11 million budget of the Civil Rights Commission to $6 million. It was also Senator Helms who befriended the developers of many "Christian academies" in North Carolina as alternatives to desegregated public schools. Early in 1982, with Helms's support, the Internal Revenue Service tried to reverse a long-standing policy requiring such schools to pay taxes.

North Carolina has the least unionized work force, one of the lowest industrial income levels, and one of the fastest-growing industrial economies in the nation.[25] It also boasts of its reputation as a harsh "law-and-order" state. Its courts give out exceptionally long sentences and the proportion of its population that is imprisoned is the highest in the nation. Before the Supreme Court decision barring capital punishment, in one year half of the entire nation's Death Row prisoners were incarcerated in Raleigh. Raleigh is also the headquarters of the National Socialist Party, whose leader, Howard Covington, drew 56,000 registered Republican votes in a statewide election recently.

Raleigh, the state capital, is also the site of a continuing federal court suit, first brought in 1971, in which fifty-one North Carolina

Agricultural Extension Service workers alleged systematic racial discrimination on the job in a federally funded agency. The U.S. Department of Justice is an intervenor on behalf of the black complainants. Similar suits were settled out of court in Texas and Louisiana and in judgments reached against Alabama and Mississippi. What is exceptional in North Carolina is the protractedness of the defense. The city of Greensboro was the site during 1981 of a dramatic trial of Nazi Party and Ku Klux Klan members accused of murdering Communist Workers' Party marchers during an otherwise peaceful demonstration.

In other words, North Carolina is a state of stunning contrasts and contradictions, as it has been since colonial times. Today, those contrasts bear far more dramatically on national events than they did in earlier periods, however, for North Carolina has become an industrial giant, a locus for multinational corporate expansion, and a prime mover in the political as well as economic emergence of the New South. And, in the course of living through its internal contradictions, North Carolina carries its diverse positions to greater extremes than do other states, as we shall show in the analysis of the *Adams* case. It also discloses more about the policies and cross-pressures shared by it and other states than can be seen from the actions of others.

The precipating circumstances in the North Carolina case suggest the abundant contradictions underlying equity issues in higher education. For example, in 1957, the North Carolina General Assembly eliminated race as a basis for determining the missions or admissions policies of any of the state's higher education institutions. This compliance with *Brown* came just two years after formation of a State Board of Higher Education, itself a sign of movement to end a racially dual system.

By 1965, a handful of black students were enrolled in every TWI, and some campuses such as Chapel Hill began to recruit and aid black students by 1967. When the pressure from the *Adams* litigations was first applied, North Carolina (whether for that reason or for reasons of its own, or both) began to reorganize its public colleges, and in 1971 the first step toward a unified system of university campuses was taken. At that important turning point, the new Board of Governors committed itself to expanding opportunities for black students and to encouraging "further racial integration of the student populations."

One cannot comprehend later events without understanding that UNC, as a racially dual but centralized system, came into being between 1963 and 1973. (Table 1–1 summarizes the UNC system.) Before that, the pattern was confined to the patchwork evolution of

Table 1-1
The Institutional Campuses of the University of North Carolina

Type[1]	Name	Location	Abbreviation	Racial Designation[2]
General Baccalaureate	University of North Carolina at Asheville	Asheville	UNC-A	TWI
	University of North Carolina at Wilmington	Wilmington	UNC-W	TWI
	Pembroke State University	Pembroke	PSU	TWI
	Fayetteville State University	Fayetteville	FSU	TBI
	Winston-Salem State University	Winston-Salem	WSSU	TBI
	Elizabeth City State University	Elizabeth City	ECSU	TBI
Comprehensive	Western Carolina University	Colluwhee	WCU	TWI
	University of North Carolina at Charlotte	Charlotte	UNC-C	TWI
	North Carolina Central University	Durham	NCCU	TBI
	North Carolina Agricultural and Technical State University	Greensboro	NC/A&T	TBI
Doctoral & Other	Appalachian State University	Boone	ASU	TWI
	East Carolina University	Greenville	ECU	TWI
	North Carolina State University	Raleigh	NCSU	TWI
	University of North Carolina at Greensboro	Greensboro	UNC-G	TWI
	University of North Carolina at Chapel Hill	Chapel Hill	UNC-Ch	TWI

Note: University of North Carolina School of the Arts has been excluded from this table, as it was from the trial of 1980–1981, because of its programmatic uniqueness.

[1]The American Council of Education classifies institutions as to scope of offerings and levels of degree programs: *General baccalaureate* institutions offer mainly B.A. and B.S. degree programs. *Comprehensive* institutions offer B.A. and B.S. degrees plus master's and some professional degrees (e.g., NCCU has law degree and library degree programs). *Doctoral* institutions offer all of the above plus Ph.D. and M.A. programs. ASU is other.

[2]TWI = Traditionally White Institution; TBI = Traditionally Black Institution. Classification designated during *Adams.*

some campuses and a kind of stunting of others. North Carolina Agricultural and Technical State University (A&T) had been created hastily in 1891, for instance, in order to comply with an 1890 amendment to the Morrill Act which declared that land grant colleges could not exclude blacks unless a state set up a separate land grant college for blacks. The private, black Shaw University set up temporary quarters for A&T on its campus, thus preserving federal funding for nearby white North Carolina State University.

Four new white campuses of the university system came into the network after 1963. Moreover, in 1963, and for the next ten years, three of those four were funded to an extent that greatly outdistanced any of the TBIs. Fayetteville State was created, for example, to train black teachers in 1877, but it did not become a four-year degree campus until 1939. Fayetteville, in fact, only became part of the UNC system in 1972.

UNC expanded swiftly and became centralized in a period when competition between the states for such growth was intensifying severely. The aim of state university presidents in the years between 1960 and 1972 was to multiply campuses and to have more than a single elite or flagship institution among them. In the pell-mell movement toward this aim, long-neglected black colleges had no creditability. Rickety, cheaply constructed facilities from the 1890–1930 period could hardly compete for renewal with the exciting politics of new campus construction.

The new TWI campus begun in Wilmington in the 1960s is a gleaming gem of architectural ingenuity, designed to create an aesthetic impression of a campus built by Thomas Jefferson himself. The facilities of the UNC School of the Arts, begun in 1963, made the 1897 campus of the TBI, Winston-Salem State University, only a few miles away, look decrepit—although some new buildings were added after 1976. Charlotte, the fastest growing commercial metropolis in the Carolinas, had no public college. It was the home of Johnson C. Smith University, a church-sponsord black school,[26] but the new TWI campus of Charlotte was erected far out in suburbia, where future expansion into a world class university could be assured.

The *Adams* decision put the brakes to this approach to resource allocation. After 1973, state system planning became more cautious. Extra aid was meted out to the TBIs, but in a way that did not impede continuing, public investments in the new TWIs. When a new medical school was planned, for example, it was assigned to East Carolina State University, formed as a normal school for whites in 1909 but developed by 1965 into the third largest campus in the UNC system.

The development of UNC as a state *system* and the resources for its expansion during the 1963–1973 decade were in part by-products of the great enlargement of federal funding in that period. That funding carried with it sets of regulatory procedures that encouraged increased emphasis on planning and management efficiency. Thus, campuses came to be categorized according to missions and so-called service areas. UNC's General Administration classified three of the five TBIs as "general baccalaureate" schools serving their geographic locale; the other two were defined as "comprehensive universities." Chapel Hill, North Carolina State, East Carolina, and Greensboro were named as graduate universities. Funds were allocated in part according to mission classification.

The great paradox for North Carolina following *Adams* was that its earlier failure—that of building a racially dual network of desegregated campuses—was then compounded. Very heavy investments in several TWIs, begun in the 1960s, persisted as plans laid in that expansionary decade became political pledges. As a result, the gap between the TBIs and the TWIs widened, even though some extra aid went to the TBIs. The funding pattern for campuses had become fairly fixed, and rationalizations became an urgent necessity.

THE ROLE OF THE FEDERAL GOVERNMENT IN EDUCATION

Myths woven by anti-federalist leaders have created a widely shared public impression that education at all levels is an institution whose policies and practices are determined by the states. When one adds to this myth the idea that colleges and universities are uniquely autonomous, almost quasi-sacred institutions set apart from the spokes as well as the rim of the commonwealth, the impression is created of a near vacuum of governmental control.

The truth of both matters is that federal government intervention in education at all levels has always been substantial. Part of it follows the tradition of federalism, which contains strong customs of federal-state-local government partnerships, mutually developed. Another part stems from the assertion of constitutional powers. Every President from George Washington to Ronald Reagan has advocated for or administered one federally funded investment or another of vast importance to American education.

The national emergency of war—civil, hot, and cold alike—has been the driving force behind the largest and most enduring of all federal investments in education. In spite of fears about a standing army, for example, lessons learned from the problems encountered in building the Continental Army led to creation of the U.S. Military Academy at West Point in 1802. The land grant colleges funded by the Morrill Act on the eve of the Civil War were, in the afterglow of that war, mandated and funded to teach military science.

World War I produced the Smith-Hughes Act (1917) to build technical and vocational training programs, including teacher training at normal schools. The GI Bill and subsequent educational benefits grew out of World War II. The National Defense Education Act (1958)—the first really vast federal outlay—grew out of the perceived dangers of the cold war.

Federal investments in state and local education took off on their greatest upward spiral not in 1965, when the Elementary and Secondary Education Act (ESEA) was passed, but in 1956, on the eve of President Dwight Eisenhower's advocacy for the National Defense Education Act (NDEA). Over the years from 1956 to 1965, annual federal funding of educational programs rose from $400 million to $2.4 billion. Total appropriations for education, training, and related programs leaped upward from $2.6 billion to $7.2 billion a year. Again, this period reflects the impacts of the Korean Conflict and the challenge imposed by the Soviet launching of Sputnik.

In 1965, the Administration of President Lyndon Johnson and the Congress greatly accelerated the spiral of federal aid. For a brief time, the national defense element was transmuted into the War on Poverty. So great was the scope of increased aid, however, that states had to struggle to adapt to the magnitude. By 1969, for example, an estimated two-thirds of all state education staffs were funded by Title V of ESEA and related categorical programs in the same act, together with the greatly expanded Vocational Education Act.

These changes after 1965 also caused a significant change in the nature of the federal role in the education delivery system. The old passive role of either providing general aid or fully funding selected, small-scale projects (e.g., the science education programs) gave way as the federal government became much more active in seeking to influence the expenditure of state and local, as well as federal, funds. This change is reflected in the rapid increase in the number of separate federal programs. Correspondingly, this change can be seen in the growth in size and complexity of HEW.

The environment of state universities was transformed under the impact of federal aid. Power has begun to centralize quite rapidly.[27] As states have presided over the actions of campuses, moreover, they have done so across a half-century of expansion in the scale, demographic size, and complexity of educational delivery systems— an expansion stimulated and guided by federal aid. In coping with expansion, states have intensified their own levels of bureaucratization. This organizational change brought with it a concentration of power.

Over the past twenty-five years, we have moved from a relatively stagnant period of spending, through a period of considerable growth and readily available revenues, to a period of increasing fiscal austerity. Correspondingly, legislative mandates and administrative guidelines for managing expenditures on campuses have together become the very center of policy life there.

From the great success of the GI Bill beginning in 1946 until about 1973, all attention in public higher education tended to be riveted to the goal of expanding access.[28] College-going changed in those years from something that 20 percent of each crop of eighteen-year-olds did to something for 30 to 40 percent of them. State universities became part of the total *mass* service system of the nation, although some campuses remained selective.

When the period of expanding access ended, the goal of *efficiency* came to replace the goal of opportunity. This change was reinforced substantially by federal grant and aid requirements for planning and detailed accountability. And when inflation pressed down with overwhelming force after Vietnam, the ideals of expanding access and efficiency began to congeal into a simple objective of distributing state resources in a kind of mechanically exact manner across state campuses. Thus, colleges that did not expand before 1973 were locked into their second- and third-class positions.

A closely related concern, which in recent years has become a major issue on many campuses, is the degree to which federal programs "leverage" college funds (i.e., in order to receive a given amount of federal monies, some amount—often much larger—of state monies must be expended in a federally specified way). This leveraging can take a variety of forms. Direct federal funding represents a small part of most colleges' budgets, but the total federal impact on those budgets is considerably greater.

Current federal legislation has evolved considerably from the orientation to curriculum of the late 1950s and the focus on the provision of specific services of the early 1960s. Federal legislation for a time tried to ensure that a significant portion of federal monies were expended on selected subpopulations such as veterans, women, minorities, and the handicapped. Similarly, today's aid carries with it elaborate reporting requirements to ensure that funds are spent on certain target populations. This focus in federal legislation has increased the concentration of federal monies on selected colleges and target populations. Thus, while the overall federal share of funding remains at less than 10 percent, federal dollars represent a much larger share of the funding for some colleges.

And, since 1965, educational policy and practice have become a major source of litigation and judicial review. This involvement has been reinforced by the changing social role of colleges, stemming in part from the tremendous growth of the education sector and in part from the evolution of civil rights legislation and litigation.

The same university trustees and officers who complain that their campuses are choking with governmental regulation and red tape also compete very vigorously for federal investments in higher education. As the big money pools of the 1965–1975 period dry up, the dependence on government aid escalates even as the pressure for freedom from federal constraints intensifies. Control over state university budgets becomes a severe preoccupation. The myth of the "new federalism," a contradiction in terms given the long history of federalism, promises to send the money—less of it, perhaps—without the regulatory restraints.

Thus, as UNC after 1973 faced into HEW's demands based on *Adams*, its board members and officers groped for a way to keep UNC's $100 million a year in federal aid, but to keep it free from Title VI regulations. No one explored the question of whether desegregation could be coupled with increased efficiency, because the answer could lead to reduced budgets for some of the most prestigious campuses, as we shall show.

In Conclusion

We have now set the historical stage for the analytical chapters that follow. We have explained the background of the *Adams* case, the most vital decision since *Brown* in the annals of American higher education, and seen how the case, decided in 1973, continues to flare as a major dispute in North Carolina. This chapter has also framed the issue of racial injustice in public higher education, showing how the federal government has accumulated heavy responsibility for regulatory enforcement of civil rights in higher education—a development that is consistent with two centuries of federal-state partnerships in education.

Inasmuch as there once was a state law—lifted twenty-five years ago— *requiring* racial segregation in North Carolina's public colleges, the issue of what remains unjust and what can be done to remedy those wrongs becomes very complex. It relies for its delineation on matters more subtle than the rights of students to apply, to gain admission, and to enroll in a college where a different racial group is dominant. Chapters Two, Three, and Four analyze those complexities.

NOTES

1. *Brown v. Board of Education of Topeka*, 347 U.S.483 (1954).

2. Gunnar Myrdal, *An American Dilemma*, Harper and Bros.: New York, 1944.

3. *Missouri ex.rel. Gaines v. Canada*, 305 U.S.337 (1938).

4. *Sweatt v. Painter*, 339 U.S.629 (1950).

5. *McLaurin v. Oklahoma State Regents*, 339 U.S.637 (1950).

6. Gail E. Thomas, ed., *Blacks in Higher Education*, Greenwood Press: Westport, Conn., 1981. Also, Carnegie Commission on Higher Education, *From Isolation to Mainstream: Problems of the Colleges Founded for Negroes*, McGraw-Hill: New York, 1971.

7. *Adams v. Richardson*, 351 F. Supp. 636, 637 (D.D.C. 1972).

8. *Adams v. Richardson*, 480 F. 2nd 1159 (D.C. Cir. 1973).

9. *Adams v. Califano*, 430 F. Supp. 118 (D.D.C. 1977).

10. *Adams v. Bell*, D.C. Civil Action No. 70-3095, footnote 39 at 13 (1982).

11. We suspect a deal was cut between Reagan and Helms on both this case and on the tax status of Bob Jones University prior to the November 1981 presidential election, but this is speculative.

12. *Adams v. Bell*, D.C. Civil Action No. 70-3095, footnote 39 at 47 (1982).

13. Thomas, *Blacks in Higher Education*, p. 11.

14. Henry A. Bullock, *A History of Negro Education in the South from 1619 to the Present*. Praeger: New York, 1967.

15. Thomas, *Blacks in Higher Education*, p. 13.

16. Ibid., p. 14.

17. See, for example, Frank Bowler and Frank A. DeCosta, *Between Two Worlds: A Profile of Negro Higher Education*. McGraw-Hill: New York, 1971.

18. Thomas, *Blacks in Higher Education*, pp. 336–355.

19. *Bakke v. Regents of the University of California*, No. 76-811 (1978).

20. Letter from National Association for Equal Opportunity in Higher Education (NAFEO) to Director, Office for Civil Rights, 1980. Also see Charles V. Willie and Marlene Y. MacLeish, "Priorities of Black College Presidents," *Educational Record*, Vol. 57, Spring 1976, pp. 92–100.

21. Cleo F. Thompson, Jr., *A Comparison of Black and White Institutions of Higher Education in North Carolina*, Doctoral dissertation, Duke University,

1977; and Gregory Kannerstein, *A Comparative Study of Certain Selected Characteristics of Black and White Public Colleges in the Same City*, Doctoral dissertation, Harvard Graduate School of Education, 1979.

22.   Charles V. Smith, "Problems and Possibilities of the Predominantly Negro College," *Journal of Social and Behavioral Sciences*, Vol. 13, Fall 1968, pp. 3–8; Elias Blake, Jr., "Future Leadership Roles for Predominantly Black Colleges and Universities in Higher Education," *Daedalus*, 100, Summer 1971, pp. 745–771.

23.   *Craig v. Alabama State University*, 451 F.Supp. 1207 (1978), p. 213.

24.   Kannerstein, *A Comparative Study*.

25.   W. W. Finlator, "Civil Liberties in North Carolina," *The Churchman*, October 1981, pp. 6–7. Our paragraph relies upon Dr. Finlator's address delivered at the Frank Graham Memorial Banquet in Raleigh, North Carolina.

26.   Arthur A. Georger, *The History of Johnson C. Smith Univerity*, Doctoral dissertation, New York University, 1954.

27.   Barry M. Richman and Richard N. Farmer, *Leadership, Goals, and Power in Higher Education*, Jossey-Bass: San Francisco, 1974; and Chester D. McCorkle, Jr. and Sandra O. Archibald, *Management and Leadership in Higher Education*, Jossey-Bass: San Francisco, 1982.

28.   Robert M. Hauser and David L. Featherman, "Equality of Schooling: Trends and Prospects," Sociology of Education, Vol. 49, April 1976, pp. 99–120; and Dyckman W. Vermilye, ed. *The Expanded Campus*, Jossey-Bass: San Francisco, 1972.

CHAPTER 2

The Demography of Segregation

As we noted in Chapter One, the University of North Carolina consists of sixteen campuses that offer at least the four-year B.A. and B.S. degrees. Although each had grown up somewhat independently of the others over a century of development, all sixteen were brought under the central control of a Board of Governors and a President with a staff of administrators housed near Chapel Hill in the 1960s. The trial of 1980–1981 focused by mutual agreement on fifteen of the campuses, setting aside the School for the Arts because of its programmatic uniqueness as a school devoted to preparing professional performers and support staff for orchestras, the theater, and the visual arts.

Judge Pratt had concluded in 1973 that the UNC system was racially segregated, and he had concluded in 1977 that UNC was neither planning to correct this violation of Title VI nor making progress within the plans it had formulated in 1974. This conclusion came up for reconsideration in the 1980 hearing because UNC denied its validity on the eve of termination of federal funds and because it claimed that conditions had changed since 1973, resulting in "steady progress" toward increased "cross-race enrollments." In addition, reconsideration became necessary because the hearing was to deal with the question of whether the Revised Criteria for desegregating could feasibly be implemented. Stated more simply, OCR would have to show that Title VI had been violated, that workable plans for correcting these violations could be created, and that termination of federal funds was a penalty suited to the "crime."

SEGREGATION, DESEGRATION, AND ACADEMIC FREEDOM

The violations alleged can be summed up in a single word: segregation. When the word is used in this very broad sense, it refers to several things at once, as follows:

- Students have racially unequal access to university learning opportunities.[1]

- Students, faculty, and administrators are selected or recruited and placed in some way that sequesters most of them by race.[2]

- Campuses and facilities or programs have racially identifiable features.

- A degree earned on one campus in a given program differs from comparable degrees from other campuses in the same system in terms of the level of knowledge or skill attained, in ways that are race-related.

- Resources are allocated across campuses without regard to offsetting deprivations due to longstanding policies of racial separation.

Racial segregation covers much more, in other words, than what is commonly thought of as *racial imbalance*. When we walk onto a black segregated campus, we may first note that there are four to five times more black students than we would expect to see in a state where, say, 20 percent of all public college students are black. If admission was not denied to qualified white applicants, we would need to know more than the racial proportions of the enrollment in order to infer segregation.

Enrollments by race, then, are a first point of indication—the smoke that leads one to suspect the possibility of fire. We know that the students did not get there by chance alone, that something else is at work, but that knowledge is insufficient. The broader the spectrum of indicators used, moreover, the more controversial the attributions of segregation become. University officials have become sensitive since 1960 to who gets admitted and who gets hired as faculty, but beyond these sensitivities, a numbness often sets in.

In part, this springs from the academic tradition of focusing mainly on two facets of the learning environment—student selection and faculty selection—and leaving the rest to the marketplace of licensing examinations and employability. In part, it is also an economic preference: improving access is fairly cheap, but equalizing learning environments and their instructional effects can become very costly.

The enduring tension between desegregation and university tradition was exhibited in two reports issued in 1982. In one, the Ford Foundation Commission on the Higher Education of Minorities reported that the representation of blacks, Chicanos, Puerto Ricans, and American Indians in the nation's colleges and universities had increased substantially between 1965 and 1975, but that since 1975 few gains had been made and several setbacks had occurred.[3]

The Commission recommended half a dozen remedial policies for correcting this downward trend, including changes in admissions testing, better outreach to high schools, better transfer provisions from community colleges to four-year universities, better financial aid provisions, and the development of improved academic remedial and support services at selective colleges and universities.

On February 7, 1982, Edward B. Fiske published a survey in the *New York Times* on the pace at which public colleges and universities are moving toward heightened selectivity in student admissions, using the conventional SAT measure.[4] These institutions, from California to New York, contrary to the Commission's recommendations, are reducing enrollments of students of average ability, cutting back on academic remedial and support services, and generally preparing for an era in which reductions in federal and state appropriations will force universities to decrease the number of students they serve. (In the same week, the Reagan Administration published a budget calling for deep cuts in grants for needy college students and deep cuts in guaranteed student loans. Congress rejected many of those cuts but mandated others.)

Some of those interviewed by Fiske disclosed the traditional university perspective:

> "We'd love to get out of the remedial education business," said Terry P. Roark, Chairman of Ohio State University's Council on Academic Affairs. "We were teaching material in math and science that was not college level."

> "People are operating under the fallacy that anybody should be able to get into a college," said Neil Harrington, assistant to the Chancellor of Higher Education (Massachusetts). "That's not right. A college degree is not a right in the United States Constitution."

> "A public university can be as elitist as it wants to be intellectually," said Edward D. Eddy, the provost of Penn State, "but it has no business being elitist economically or socially. To be publicly funded doesn't mean you have to be mediocre."

In its initial filing for the 1980 hearing, OCR charged that UNC had never taken sufficient action to eliminate the continuing effects of its *de jure* racially dual system; that students, faculty, administrators, and even boards of trustees were still composed and located in the segregated pattern characteristic of the pre-*Brown* era; that students at the TBIs were still getting shortchanged on quality and range of degree programs relative to students at the TWIs; and that, among other inequities, TBI plants and facilities were both older and smaller. There were other charges, but these were the major ones.

Joseph Levin responded for UNC that OCR was infringing on UNC's sacred academic freedom, grounded in the First Amendment, to determine for itself on academic grounds who may teach, what may be taught, how it shall be taught, and who may be admitted to study. He also replied that UNC had been making steady progress since 1957 toward desegregation; that no campus was closed to any student or faculty member on the basis of race; that the various campuses differed from one another as the result of differences in planned missions as well as market demands among students for types of programs.

Levin did not invent this defense. It derives from the ideas expressed in the *New York Times* survey and critiqued in the Ford Foundation Commission report. These ideas, which pervade American higher education, suggest that *stratification* by program quality, rigor of requirements, homogeneity of student abilities, and campus reputation is the basic organizing property of the university *sui generis*. If race does not in itself affect access, then the rest of Title VI reduces to the matter of self-regulation in order to prevent discrimination. All else is a part of the natural order of things academic. Racial equity, if not intentionally violated, cannot be put above academic self-determination in the pursuit of intellectual excellence. Levin's defense was broad-gauged enough to appeal to many university policymakers in every state of the union. It turned on the classic liberal tradition of racial neutrality: university decisions should be made on the bases of academic merit and individual attributes, such as student interests, not on irrelevant racial characteristics. UNC, he said in effect, was appropriately color-blind except where safeguards against discrimination had been erected.

This position seemed to account for the readiness of Morgan and Levin to take on the case, to turn the issue into a First Amendment question rather than a civil rights denial. Their position suggested that the history of UNC as a southern institution committed to equality, when compared with other institutions of higher education, would, in the eyes of both academics and lawyers, give OCR and LDF the appearance of a pair of overzealous, angry "hounds of heaven" in bellowing pursuit of an angel (Chapel Hill is often called "a little bit of heaven" by southerners).

Central to the Revised Criteria for planning compliance with Title VI was the concept of eliminating *degree program duplication* within state college systems. The idea, which had grown up out of the case law on higher education during the 1964 to 1969 period, was that in selected instances, a university system should plan to locate degree programs in such a way that the races would cross campuses in order to enroll. If two medical schools were needed in a system, for instance, and one was already based at a TWI, then the second should be based at a TBI. If a system had no school of veterinary medicine and plans were being laid for creating one, those plans should aim at a TBI in order to equalize the distribution of professional degree offerings and also to draw whites onto TBI campuses.

Morgan and Levin responded that this idea was not only a violation of academic freedom, but also was likely to have no effect because students' choice of campus hinges mainly on the congruence between their abilities and preferences: students prefer to cluster where there are students of similar level of ability and with similar program interests as well as extracurricular interests. At points, this defense against eliminating program duplication verged on the racist argument that the campuses had remained racially identifiable because blacks like to stay clustered with blacks and whites with whites, but Levin never descended to this level.

RACIAL IDENTIFIABILITY AT UNC CAMPUSES

Although OCR shared its data banks and files with us, there was much we did not know and were not equipped to find out about UNC. Relations between HEW and UNC had deteriorated by late 1979 to a point where UNC President William Friday and others had attempted to reduce, if not completely seal off, federal access to the state system's information and informed respondents.

Among the three of us, only Catherine Baltzell was born and educated in the South, and so two of us lacked any close or direct familiarity with the region, the state, and UNC. Robert Dentler, on the basis of long years of experience with school desegregation planning in northern public school districts, insisted on visiting UNC campuses firsthand before taking the witness stand as an expert, not because short tours generate valid knowledge, let alone policy wisdom, but because they do reduce the likelihood of making many small and foolish errors of fact. Richard L. Foster, assigned to serve as chief attorney for OCR for the proceeding, was sympathetic to this insistence. Born in Florida but educated at northern universities, he had come into OCR late in 1979 from the law faculty of Georgetown University. While he could rely on his own expertise as a trial lawyer, he was relying for substantive background on William E. Michaels, a North Carolinian and graduate of Chapel Hill, and on Jeffrey F. Champagne. Both attorneys had been working on the UNC case and others for some years as part of the regular OCR litigation unit.

Dentler arranged an eight-day trip to twelve of the sixteen campuses of UNC in June 1980, accompanied by his wife; Together, they toured the campuses rather like the parents of some prospective student would. Findings from the visits were included in Dentler's testimony and have been reprinted in this chapter as a means of introducing many of the UNC campuses.

What follows in this section are excerpts from the October 4, 1980 testimony of Robert Dentler [Docket Number 79-VI-1 (HUD 79-4)], who had been admitted as an expert in higher educational administration, sociology, and educational program evaluation. We are reprinting parts of pages 5439–5481 of the transcript because they introduce graphically some of the UNC campuses, particularly four of the TBIs, and because they convey the sense of what is meant by "racial identifiability."

> **Mr. Foster:** I believe that the last area of indicators or characteristics of past segregation that you mentioned yesterday involved the racial identifiability of certain characteristics of the campuses and grounds of the schools themselves. Is that correct?
>
> **Dr. Dentler:** Yes.
>
> **Mr. Foster:** Briefly, what was the basis for your opinions and conclusions in this area?
>
> **Dr. Dentler:** The opportunity to visit twelve of the fifteen campuses in June of this year.
>
> **Mr. Foster:** Why did you go?
>
> **Dr. Dentler:** I wanted to make sure that I saw for myself whether the remedial suggestions that I was beginning to model in April were feasible and that is, realistic, under the presenting conditions . . . it's not necessary to visit if you're making general recommendations or suggestions, but when you get down to concrete particulars of the kind that I was trying to go for, on course offerings, you make suggestions about course offerings and the facilities that would be required. You would need to see whether the campus could carry that, whether it would be possible to introduce that.
>
> So I was eager to visit to acquaint myself more closely [with the campuses], for that reason.

I also could not pick up enough indicators on the subject of identifiability without taking that topic with me in the course of the visit to see whether there were racially identifiable features in the setting, whether something came out.

If you say identifiability, you're talking about perception, and there are other more objective ways of doing that, and I tried to do them, but I thought that [it] would be important, since that was part of our undertaking, to see what else I could learn.

Mr. Foster: Who, if anyone, accompanied you on this tour?

Dr. Dentler: My wife.

Mr. Foster: And how long, approximately, did you spend on each of the campuses that you visited?

Dr. Dentler: We visited each of the campuses for a total of anywhere from four to six hours, depending on the scale of the campus.

Mr. Foster: How many UNC campuses did you visit?

Dr. Dentler: Twelve.

Mr. Foster: And what approach, very briefly, did you take to gathering information while on these field visits?

Dr. Dentler: I was, of course, most eager to concentrate on what I could witness and observe on the traditionally black campuses. So I stressed those.

I walked all parts of the grounds, in every instance. Toured as many of the buildings, on the interior as well as the exterior, as possible. And I spent considerable time in the administration buildings, the admissions office, the counseling offices, seeing how they were outfitted, laid out, to host and serve students, and then also studied the library collection, because I'm experienced with that, and I know how to appraise it. I've carried out that task not only in building a library in two places but in accreditation visits. A library tells you some things that are harder to learn through other means. Also, I believe that a library is expressive, profoundly expressive, of the instructional resources of any campus.

Mr. Foster: Could you briefly describe your field visits and your key observations or findings relevant to racial identifiability about the campuses you visited?

Dr. Dentler: Well, I could not fit a visit to Elizabeth City State University into the itinerary, so I made a point of going to four of the five TBIs. And of those four, the visit to North Carolina A&T was the visit most crucial to my work.

I did not realize from the documents I had that the campus site of this historic land grant university was small and that it had been built up almost to its boundaries, with the exception of the property underlying the agricultural complex.

It was important to me to witness the building of a new administration building there. It's a fairly gigantic one. What I didn't know is that there is an older administration building already in place. It is the center of the campus. I did not know that that older building, which is the gateway to the campus, was being replaced by a new structure which is on the edge of the campus, which faces outward to the highway. That seemed important to me. It's not a comment on the new building.

The old building, I also did not know, hadn't been constructed originally to house an administration. It was an old school building or an old state teachers' college. So here I had the paradox of the old structure not having been built for the housing of administrative services, yet having been somewhat adapted for that end, even though the ceilings are 20 feet high in some places, and the new administration building is not being built in a place where the in-movement and out-movement of students and faculty figures in its siting. There isn't another site, so you build on what you have.

I didn't know from the documents that the plant had been built up in a helter-skelter method; that is, over time. It's not a designed, pre-designed campus.

I did not know that the construction of the buildings going back to the nineteenth century was of such poor quality. Many of the structures are as old as I learned they were from the facilities reports. I didn't know from those reports how well cleaned they were. I also didn't know that the site is in a black, working-class residential section of Greensboro, and that the agriculture complex is really something on the edge of Greensboro, set well apart from the campus. It amounts to a—it would be called a marginal family farm of 1900 or 1910, in its scale.

Mr. Foster: When you say it, you're referring to the—

Dr. Dentler: The agricultural facilities. The amount of land and the few buildings that comprise it. The environmental studies setup at North Carolina A&T which I'd looked forward to visiting consists of a small prefab building set up on a farmer's conservation pond across the street from the barn. And I couldn't find any other traces of the environmental studies complex beyond that.

The education school, while the building was constructed in 1954, turned out to have been designed exactly like many junior high schools were designed in 1940. I've been in hundreds of them around the country. And you can't expand the thing. It's got low ceilings, two-floor structure, fixed space.

All the staff and faculty offices are on the first floor and on the second floor there are a series of little boxes, small, square classrooms, with chairs in a row. By the way, summer session was in operation, so I was able to see the faculty and staff and students present.

I was fascinated to learn from the materials from the Admissions Office that summer term had begun on May 4 at North Carolina A&T, and the explanation was that everyone needs to get back to the farms. So they had a schedule which differs from the other campuses and is tied to a time when you had agrarian rhythms of planting and getting crops ready for later harvests. That also, of course, means that people graduate at the end of April at A&T. It has its own unique rhythms.

I also found . . . the library collection where I checked the collection in art, English literature and the government documents room. It is a repository for government documents. And I checked the sociology collection. All except the sociology collection concentrated on materials from the 1920s and '30s. That is, three out of four of the books in each of the subject matter areas that I sampled began to—were from the 1920 to 1930 period. The sociology collection, by contrast, was adequate.

The government documents may have been in some basement room and out of reach. But the most recent government documents I could sample from the shelves were from the 1950s. The library is extraordinarily well staffed. I found one student on the four floors of the stacks. But I found fifteen staff members at work in the building.

I also had an opportunity to visit the Afro-American Museum at North Carolina A&T which has some very distinguished African objets d'art and would constitute a front-ranking exhibit in collections that I've seen elsewhere. However, it's in a very, very tiny building. That is, the entire museum is smaller than this courtroom. The visitors' register and the gracious museum director both made plain that about three people a week visit the museum.

The visit to A&T shook me. I wanted to find out whether it was like the catalog that I had read and liked. I had to reach the conclusion that this was not a campus that could be built up, that its programs, to be remedied, would have to be modified and redesigned. There is no place to launch a series of new programs on that site. And the contrast between the levels of quality if you put in new facilities for instruction and the old ones would present a grave contradiction and would generate some new kinds of inequalities. You would have some students attending facilities in the agriculture program where the silo approximates the Tower of Pisa and you would have—

Mr. Levin: Objection, Your Honor. I move to strike. I haven't the slightest idea what the witness means by that. And if he's going to give a professional judgment about something it seems to me that the witness should give a professional judgment without mischaracterizations.

Judge Mathias: Let's see what you mean by the Tower of Pisa, Dr. Dentler. And would you please explain your comment on the record?

Dr. Dentler: Yes. The silo next to the barn leans at a slight angle which is not part of the original design.

Judge Mathias: All right. You may proceed.

Dr. Dentler: The students in older more established programs, such as agriculture, would be hosted and served alongside students in a program that had been fitted into new facilities. And you would have serious strains set up between departments and majors.

Mr. Foster: Were there other key findings and conclusions that had relevance to you as a result of your A&T visit?

Dr. Dentler: The conclusion I reached from the field visit to the A&T campus was that resources had not come in over its full history in a continuous or steady fashion—that periodically some new structures had been built or some old ones renovated. But there were discontinuities there.

A&T, by the way, was one of the schools that explained on the telephone that no catalogs were available and that they had been out of stock since January. I was visiting in June and the Admissions Officer explained that they were still out of stock and that they hoped to have new catalogs in September. There was no other literature available depicting the programs that you could get on request.

The other thing that I noticed that I couldn't learn from the documents was that landscape sculptures have been built by black fraternities. And that these dot the grounds around the central administration. These structures I would call what an anthropologist would call them, I believe, and that is totemic displays.

They are wooden carved dogs and other animals that are totems from the black fraternal organizations. And the reason that's important is that there were two criteria [for displaying sculpture] in the University administration, neither of which had been observed here.

One is if you have works of sculpture displayed on the campus grounds then you have to reach some aesthetic standard. These were not works of art. These are local ceremonial objects. No group had led to the selection of them.

Secondly, there's another criterion and that is that if you have special interest group displays on a campus, whether it's fraternal or religious or political, you agree in advance on where those special interest displays and communications can be displayed.

For example, at the University of California at Berkeley, very, very firm rules were established about where tables and displays of political groups could be laid out.

Mr. Levin: Your Honor, I'm going to object to this unless the witness is going to link it up to something relevant.

Mr. Foster: I think you're—

Judge Mathias: Well, I'm going to overrule the objection. You may proceed.

Mr. Foster: If you would, Dr. Dentler, summarize what, if any, pertinence these particular totemic displays that you observed have to your conclusions about racial identifiability or indicators of past segregation.

Dr. Dentler: The displays on the central campus of A&T said to me that the campus was distinctively to be identified with those black fraternities. And that is not a universalistic message. That's not an invitation that's inclusive or welcoming to groups, either non-fraternity members or nonblack visitors and students, faculty and staff.

And that's why I brought it up. Like other visitors to the region, I am sure they [would feel] particular intensification of the impressions from the visit by the subsequent visit to the Greensboro campus which is within the same city and just a very few miles away.

Mr. Foster: Could you briefly summarize your observations, particularly your key summary conclusions about any comparisons between Greensboro and A&T that were of relevance to you?

Dr. Dentler: Yes. In sharp contrast, I found that UNC Greensboro has a hillside setting whch is very, very similar to the campus of Chapel Hill. And it has ample room on that setting for further expansion. That the campus, itself, is built into the wealthiest white residential sector of an industrial city.

The campus site simply occupies a different world, ecologically, from the site of North Carolina A&T, though they are in the same urban city. The splendid new buildings at Greensboro have come to rim the campus core, which is itself old, and has much grace and visual beauty.

Mr. Foster: Would you continue to briefly describe your visits and briefly summarize your key observations about the campuses you saw as those observations relate to racial identifiability or characteristics of past segregation?

Dr. Dentler: In contrast to A&T, North Carolina Central's campus turned out to be a highly developed campus with many large excellently maintained and well-designed buildings. Two-thirds of the buildings having been built since 1965. From having long experience in it, it was my note that evening that I thought the plant, that is the grounds and the buildings of Central, were in the best kept condition of any that I've ever seen.

And the law building under construction shows careful planning so that the old law building, which is very small, will emerge to be a library with support offices. And the new building will contain all other activities. The new law building could—I have been told in the documents that it was projected for some growth. But the emerging layout could handle a doubling of the student scale of that law school. So it's built with an eye to the future.

The library is also new. It's very large. It's well built. And it has a bigger staff. In the basic book collection, far from being a set of books left over from the '30s and '20s, it's solid and there's a great deal of space for future acquisitions.

The dormitories appear to be excellent structures with fine close-in sites. That is, you can live there and get to and from the campus classrooms with great ease. The campus setting, while it is in a black residential neighborhood, is economically integrated as a middle-class section.

And there's a very well-built housing project about eight blocks away. And I also was influenced by discovering that Central has a nearly brand new superb communications facility. And since I had been verging on remedial designs for emphasizing public communications at Central, I realized the magnificent foresight of the administration and here it was. It already has in it the language departments and related communications offerings. It's waiting to become a public communications center.

The social science book collection, the public administration collections are very strong. Central could, given a coherence of mission statement, break out of its history as a black college and a normal school with ease. And the scale of the plant could readily sustain expansion of students. And graduate emphasis, consolidation of programs there, would make Central clearly magnetic. So I didn't understand it before.

Mr. Foster: Would you continue summarizing your observations about the campuses you visited?

Dr. Dentler: I visited Winston-Salem. And, again, my long-distance assumptions from reading were challenged. Winston-Salem's campus is not downtown at all. It is three miles from the center of the central business district of the region.

It is on a well laid out but very small island land plot next to two sets of railroad tracks which border two sides of the campus. There are no shops or other retail services nearby. But there is ease of bus commuting right on the campus, about a ten-minute bus trip to and from other parts of Winston-Salem.

Winston-Salem can't be expanded. But it's well designed. It's built up with many sound new buildings including a good library, a good student center, a big communications building, and so forth. Everything there—it was in the middle of summer school as well—was clean and new and in heavy use.

What you get, if you're an educationally seasoned visitor, is the impression that you're visiting an ideal little liberal arts college that anyone could go to. The library reinforces that. And I checked out a series of the same collections there and found that they were strong. The government documents room is exemplary and right up to date; right up to the minute. The library staff was most helpful there in showing how they were organized.

Everything in the new communications building, which has multimedia classrooms, an amphitheater for lectures, a writing laboratory, everything is excellent in design and construction but it's small. The same thing is true of the Student Union.

And the only really big structure on the campus is the administration building. The land site is such that you can't expand it. It doesn't mean you might not have a satellite campus somewhere or an adjacent program somewhere. But the total land site is not going to host more than 2,500 students. This is not a college that can become a real comprehensive university.

It does seem to me from the visit that it would have a good chance to desegregate. The city doesn't have strong competing colleges except for the UNC–School of the Arts which draws from a nationwide applicant pool. But the city has prosperity and the region has the viability to supply a very sizeable college-bound population.

So the only thing that seems to stand in the way of Winston-Salem emerging and becoming a magnetic competitive undergraduate baccalaureate college is its history as a black state teachers' college. And there isn't room to expand very much, as I noted before.

Again, the history is very visible in the same totemic displays as on the A&T campus, ringing the same kind of administration building. The black fraternity sculptures and fraternity letters are neither universal art nor racially neutral displays if they occupy a prominent place in the very middle of the campus.

So Winston-Salem could be desegregatively very viable. Right now, it looks set apart. It still has the earmarks of racial identifiability within that city.

Mr. Foster: Continuing again, would you just briefly summarize your conclusions and your appropriate illustrations of your observations from your visits?

Dr. Dentler: In each city I went to I made a point of asking people, although I had a map and knew how to get to the campus in a rental car, I tried to stop and ask people how you got to the State University as part of a simple test of whether people knew about the State University and considered it as something they could refer you to.

When I got to Fayetteville, I did that after dinner. I asked the restaurant cashier and the waitress standing next to her the way to the University of North Carolina at Fayetteville and both of these white women shook their heads.

The waitress said to me, "There isn't any such school. I wish there was. Because if there was I would like to take some courses." And then a middle-aged black man behind me at the cashier's line looked up and smiled and said, "Well, what are you looking for?"

I said, "Well, I've come a long, long way to see the State University campus." And he said, "I can tell you." And the waitress said, "Well, we can't tell you how to get there."

Mr. Levin: Your Honor, I thought that for some small portion of this there might be some relevance. But I did not realize we were getting into an extended hearsay conversation which sounds like the dialogue for a television sitcom. So I object to that.

Mr. Foster: Your Honor, I think it's very illustrative of one type of technique Dr. Dentler used to—

Judge Mathias: All right. I'm going to overrule the objection. But I would ask him to shorten the story.

Mr. Foster: Dr. Dentler, if you could briefly complete that last anecdote and then summarize your conclusions about Fayetteville State.

Dr. Dentler: Well, the cashier simply said, "We can't tell you how to get there but Captain Jim over here can." She pointed to the black gentleman and he explained to me how to get to Fayetteville State.

Mr. Foster: And what are your basic conclusions from your observations at Fayetteville State?

Dr. Dentler: That I hadn't known that it is built on what plaintiffs would call railroad land. That a railroad still in use runs across the campus, has pathways across it for students. That it's based in a black neighborhood of Fayetteville—

Mr. Foster: Let me stop you there for a moment. What, if any, significance did those two facts have for you in terms of your opinions about indicators or characteristics of past segregation? The two facts I'm referring to are the fact that Fayetteville was built on railroad land and was in a black residential neighborhood.

Dr. Dentler: Well, that the possibilities for surmounting its history as a black teachers' college are physically limited. That a visitor would conclude that this site has some characteristics which are not racially neutral.

Mr. Foster: And of the five TBIs, how many, if you know, are in black residential neighborhoods?

Dr. Dentler: I won't presume to speak for Elizabeth City. But the four I visited are. At Fayetteville and A&T, you have to go some distance into the black residential community before you arrive at either of those campuses.

The Fayetteville State University campus is approximately ten miles from the downtown central business district and the campus has the combined aura of a normal school and a black college. While the site is not unattractive and is exceptionally well-maintained, definite steps toward further enhancement would be needed in order to overcome the persistence of its historical identity.

There isn't anything there that was for me, as a visitor, either discouraging or a source of new hope or new possibilities. This could become a regular, multi-ethnic, four-year college. I say that because right now it's got a couple of dozen two-year degree programs. But it will need substantial enhancing and that's what I concentrated on when I took the impressions back to the drawing board.

A DEMOGRAPHIC APPROACH DEFINING RACIAL SEGREGATION AT UNC

Title VI of the Civil Rights Act does not give a working definition of the concept of racial segregation. The HEW Revised Criteria could be adapted to this purpose, but they pertain primarily to standards for gauging desegregative progress. What is more, the way they were developed and their standing as legal guidelines were both matters in dispute; hence, we drew on definitions used in the applied sociology of education in an effort to fill this gap.

These three definitions were selected, examined and applied in the course of our analyses:

1. If the majority population served by an institution (such as a public university system) is white American, then a composition of those currently being served (students) or those serving them (staff) of 51 percent black Americans offers proof of inequality in the selection process because it is not what one would find if equal chances of selection were operating.[5] Literal use of this definition can lead to the false inference that the locus of the problem lies in the proportion of black students or staff. In ad-

dition, this definition ignores the question of whether multi-ethnic composition is desirable in itself. It also invites excessive emphasis upon the statistical mechanics of racial balance, an emphasis ruled inappropriate in *Milliken v. Bradley*.[6] In spite of these limitations, the definition is serviceable as a social indicator and provides a kind of yellow flashing light to the analyst. This is particularly true for most social institutions in an overwhelmingly white majority society.

2. Sociologist Charles Willie has provided an alternative definition in his *Sociology of Urban Education*.[7] He reasons from the concept of a socially critical mass that segregation occurs when the racial minority's presence in any setting falls below a proportion of approximately 35 to 20 percent. We used 20 percent, then, as a marker of the beginnings of harm resulting from segregation. A group comprising less than 20 percent cannot exert a significant educative or policy influence over its setting.

3. A campus or school and students or staff is racially segregated, according to our third definition, derived from Robert Dentler and Mary Ellen Warshauer in *The Urban R's*,[8] if the population proportion of a given minority in the school is more than twice or less than half that in the population served by the system. For example, the percentage of black Americans enrolled on all UNC campuses in 1979 was 20 percent; a given campus would be considered segregated if its enrollment was more than 40 percent black or less than 10 percent black. Like Willie's definition, this one can be extended to multi-ethnic compositions. The rationale for the interval is that it provides reasonable tolerance for place-to-place variations resulting from chance, changes, or errors in operations.

Overview of Segregation on UNC Campuses

We found that UNC campuses were racially segregated in 1979 in every category from undergraduates, to graduate and professional students, to faculty and administrative officers, using each of our definitions. The only groups which approximated nonsegregation of students were professional students in medicine at Chapel Hill and in law at Central.

Systemwide, 20 percent of undergraduates were black, but each TBI enrolled 87 percent or more blacks in 1979 (see Appendix A, Table A–1). The TWIs enrolled 5.2 times as many undergraduates as the TBIs, yet only 7 percent were black and the total number of blacks at TWIs was far less than the number enrolled at the TBIs.

Analysis of the in-state whites entering TBIs as freshmen in 1978 revealed numbers so low as to offer no prospect of a "natural" trend toward desegregation from this critical source over the next fifty years. A&T enrolled eight white freshmen, for example. We also found in extrapolating trends that if no changes in policy or practice were made, systemwide student desegregation would occur, but not until the year 2094. We did find that there has been a slow but steady increase in student desegregation on a few TWI campuses. This trend, if extended over time, will therefore intensify desegregation at the undergraduate level. Six TWI campuses out of the ten analyzed were not making even such a slow increase, however.

Turning next to the graduate and professional student level (see Table A–2), we found that three of the five TBIs had no graduate programs, whereas two of the three "general baccalaureate" TWIs had already grown small master's degree groups. Nearly half of all post-baccalaureate students for all campuses are concentrated at Chapel Hill and North Carolina State (NCSU).

At Chapel Hill and at East Carolina (ECU), most black students are hosted in the medical school and allied health and life sciences programs. Law accounts for most of the whites enrolled at NCCU (Central), showing, as do the medical schools, how cross-race enrollment can benefit from the limited availability of "magnetic" degree programs. (UNC has two medical schools and two law schools.)

The level of segregation on a campus often gets established in the aftermath of decisions made by the Board of Governors and its General Administration. UNC–Greensboro was a small white women's teachers college until 1963. In 1973, the Board began to build that campus as a major doctoral studies center to be added to Chapel Hill and North Carolina State. While A&T languished three miles away on the "black side" of the city, UNC–Greensboro became in one decade a second Chapel Hill. Most universities tend to "grow" graduate programs, but rarely at this pace. A&T never got to grow a single doctoral program in its ninety-year history.[9]

Problems of Mission

All of the TWIs have planned, highly explicit missions. These are used in student and faculty recruitment, program development proposals, and the planning of facilities. Three of the five TBIs do not have clear missions, however. Bachelor's degrees granted by all UNC campuses are summarized in Table A–3.

A&T is neither agricultural nor technological in the main, for example, but rather centers on teacher education. Fayetteville's 103 years in teacher preparation have left an indelible mark. A "normal school" type of curriculum is required for all undergraduates in the first four terms. It includes Basic Grammar, Personal Hygiene, Physical Education, and Reading. Majors have been built up in recent years at the junior-senior level in several fields outside education, mostly in zoology, policy science, business, and computer applications. Then, too, there are twenty-three two-year Associate of Arts programs offered. Thus, Fayetteville is a state normal school for elementary and middle-school teachers, a junior college, *and* a multipurpose campus that is evolving slowly into the arts, sciences, and business. In the arts, music courses abound but most of them are offered under music education.

Demographic Segregation of Faculty

Analysis of the racial composition of full-time faculty on each campus revealed that all five TBIs have unsegregated faculties, but that these five schools account for 565 of the 706 black professors employed on all fifteen UNC campuses. *Slow progress* in the recruitment of black faculty into TWIs since 1974 suggests that, based on extrapolation of current rates, it would take until the year 2083 to reach 10 percent black faculty at the TWIs. (Tables A–4 through A–6 present data pertinent to the demographic segregation of faculty at UNC.)

The unsegregated nature of black college faculties is not a policy accomplishment of the system. Such institutions have routinely hosted white professors since 1850. Blacks were deprived of graduate study until the 1920s, with terribly few exceptions, and as late as 1980 the proportion of black doctoral graduates each year nationwide had not reached three percent of the total.[10] This circumstance—the alleged unavailability of qualified black faculty candidates—was used by UNC as an explanation of faculty segregation at TWIs, although the same unavailability had not impeded black hiring at the TBIs. But the argument has some merit, as we shall see.

Segregation of Administrative Personnel

Full-time administrative, executive, and managerial personnel were not only segregated systemwide in 1979; they were also in discriminatory flux (see Tables A–7 and A–8). Over the five-year period from 1975 to 1979, the total number of administrative personnel shrank by thirty, while whites increased by a net of seven and blacks declined by a net of thirty-seven. Expansion in number of administrative personnel has thus been limited to the TWIs and it has reinforced the racial gap.

The Board of Governors, Campus Boards of Trustees, and the staff of the General Administration are also racially segregated. The Board of Governors included 31 whites and 4 blacks—the minimum number required by statute—in 1979. The campus Boards were made up of 138 whites and 17 blacks at the TWIs, and 65 whites and 37 blacks at the TBIs. Among 43 senior administrators at General Administration headquarters, 2 were black. Among 36 other professionals at the headquarters, 3 were black in 1979.

Facilities

Although not, strictly speaking, features of demography, facilities are nevertheless indicators of the demographic differences between TWIs and TBIs. The TWIs have been built up tremendously since 1960, whereas the TBIs were erected in earlier decades. TBIs have benefitted from new construction, especially since 1970, but three of the five are the smallest, most bound-in campuses among the fifteen, and this limitation appears permanent. By virtue of age and of small outlays for rehabilitation versus large capital outlays for new construction, buildings on the TBI campuses are five times more likely to be defective than those on the TWI campuses.

In instructional facilities, every one of eight TWI campuses studied is superior to every one of the five TBIs. The contrast is most extreme at A&T, where new construction is occurring but where remodeling and rehabilitation will never catch up with new plant conditions on the TWIs. Needs for dormitory repair and replacement at A&T are equally glaring, and dormitories are twelve times more likely to be defective at TBIs than at TWIs.

These findings were based on reanalysis of data gathered by a college facilities expert, Dr. William Fuller, for OCR.[11] UNC had a study done, too, but it covered only some campuses and did not develop measures of plant quality. Fuller was unable to include the three campuses with the *best* physical facilities (Chapel Hill, North Carolina State, School of the Arts), but this simply narrowed the differences he did document very systematically.

Dentler's field visits corroborated Fuller's evidence for our team's study. He agreed with Fuller's finding that all UNC campuses are rather well built when contrasted with schools in other systems. This was the period when scandalous defects in plant construction on Massachusetts public college campuses were being investigated by a special commission, for example. Even A&T, with its many outworn structures from the 1895–1920 era, was well maintained, and new buildings were being erected.

MODELING FEASIBLE DESEGREGATION

In our judgment, the pattern of racial separation among students, faculty, and administrators was highly consistent if incomplete proof that UNC remains a segregated, racially dual state system. The pattern is reinforced by the manifest racial identifiability of some campuses, and by the buildup of TWI plants relative to TBI plants. Other evidence is offered in Chapters Three and Four.

The response of UNC to this evidence was that it is the result of academic market trends, student preferences, and variable initiatives exerted by the individual campuses. Part of the response also was that the TWIs are gradually gaining black enrollments anyway and that the plan of UNC is to safeguard the availability of opportunities for the maximum numbers of students of both races.

UNC's plans from 1974 through 1980 are noteworthy for the absence of *explicitly* desegregative strategies for this reason and because such concerns, which are necessarily race-based, are not part of the racially neutral orientation of the system's planning process. That neutrality is not comprehensive, however. UNC has aided black students financially in support of desegrating the TWIs, and it funds doctoral studies for a few black faculty each year, for example. It has also upgraded TBI libraries and added new buildings in a belated effort to be more equitable.

Our task therefore became one of developing models of desegregation in order to fill in the blanks left by UNC's plans and in order to estimate how much effort would be required to desegregate all campuses between 1981 and 1990. The year 1990 was chosen because some reasonable yet prompt dateline had to be set if the principle of remedying a longstanding wrong was to be followed. If a remedy could not be implemented within eight years, we reasoned, then its basic feasibility should be challenged.

Desegregation of Undergraduate Students

We assumed an overall growth in undergraduate students from 92,489 in 1979 to 97,679 in 1990, based on enrollment estimates made by demographers for UNC. We further assumed that the proportion of blacks would rise from 20 to 26 percent, based on the same estimates *and* on improved recruitment efforts. Finally, we set an outer limit of 51 percent black (following the first definition of segregation given above) and an inner limit of 13 percent black (one-half of 26 percent, following the third definition given above) and applied it to each campus. Appalachia State (ASU) in the western mountain region, for example, cannot realistically draw more than 13 percent black students, given the in-state residential distribution. (We assumed that the proportion of foreign students would remain roughly consistent with 1979 figures.) Table A–9 presents goals for undergraduate desegregation by campus.

We then asked what actions would be required to accomplish undergraduate student desegregation. In order to answer that question, we had initially to test what the results would be if the trends since 1975 were simply projected forward to 1990, without changes in policies or practices. Our major realization from this statistical exercise was that the five TBIs would become depopulated! This would result from the currently accelerating rates of entry of black undergraduates into six of the ten TWIs. The terrible irony is that, without other desegregative actions, the TBIs could be preserved until 1990 under only one of two conditions: either *de jure* segregation would have to be reintroduced (a moral, legal, and political impossibility), or TBIs would have to find ways to recruit students denied admission elsewhere in the system because of grave educational deficiencies.

It is easy to understand how depopulation of the TBIs will occur. Chapel Hill, State, East Carolina, and Charlotte are each nearly twice as big as A&T, the largest TBI. As blacks move in increasing numbers into these schools, the numerical impact is severe. A 2 percent increase at Chapel Hill, for example, equals nearly 300 black students; the TBI at Elizabeth City (ECSU) admits only 300 black freshmen each year now, along with 30 whites.

We found that policy changes powerful enough to retain black students *and* accelerate enrollment of new white students in TBIs by three times the 1979 rate was the minimum essential to achieve desegregation.

Our analysis led us to devise four remedial policies to augment changes already underway at the TBIs. First, we found that TBIs have a relatively weak hold on white undergraduates, who tend to transfer out after their first and second years. Retention practices involving welcoming, assisting, and supporting whites would have to be upgraded. We also found that *financial aid* for whites with low family resources would make an important difference in recruiting freshmen. And, we found that TBIs lack the capacity for effective *outreach* into the white residential areas of the state and that their capacity falls far below the several TWIs that now reach out to black students.

Even with these three changes, we found that TBIs could be desegregated only if degree programs were *consolidated* across some of the campuses (see Table A–10). This remedy had been used already with some success in Tennessee and Alabama, and it was being planned in other states. The Revised Criteria for implementing Title VI refer to it as the "planful elimination of program duplication." What it means is that if degree programs in high demand are located at black colleges but are not available in duplicate at some of the eleven white colleges, cross-race redistributions will be stimulated.

To explore consolidation, we identified nine essential fields and studied their current extent of duplication. For example, UNC currently offers nursing on nine campuses, three of them TBIs. (The latter programs were threatened by the Board of Governors in 1979 with termination unless more of their graduates, nearly all of them black, began to pass the professional licensing exam.) We proposed to limit the nursing programs to four campuses, Winston-Salem and Central because they are TBIs, and Chapel Hill and East Carolina, because they have medical schools and teaching hospitals. The effect would be to enlarge, upgrade, and desegregate the two black student bodies. The A&T program—the only program to be dropped at a TBI—would be discontinued as the weakest and least essential in the system.

Similar actions were suggested for eight other popular degree programs offering marketable degrees. Sites for consolidation were selected after analysis of current offerings, service regions, and scale of future demand. We also recommended phasing in each consolidation over three years, in order to serve students enrolled as of 1982. We gave evidence to show, finally, that consolidation could generate dollar savings, which could in turn fund improvements in remaining programs. We estimated that the entire process would reduce faculty positions overall by no more than twenty-five.

No action we proposed met stiffer or more outraged opposition than this one. Although state systems often relocate programs and terminate others, a variety of academic experts testified that this is *always* done to improve degree program quality, extend opportunity, or at worst, to cope with budgetary exigencies. It should never be done in order to desegregate, said experts testifying for UNC, it can only be done after long planning on the campuses and work by systemwide committees. Even then, they argued, consolidation would not affect segregation because students do not choose B.A. and B.S. programs for career or academic interests but because they decide to enroll at a certain campus. That choice is not a function of course offerings or major fields, said these experts, but is a function of seeking out a peer group with common interests and school achievement levels. Hence, to consolidate is to damage this "natural" self-selection and to throw lower-ability students, presumed to be mainly blacks, into competition with abler students, to the detriment of blacks.

In our opinion, based on a review of the literature on college choice and retention,[12] one of these arguments has merit: a plan to consolidate degree programs is best devised from *within* universities, where the multivariate considerations can all be taken into account. What is more, only this kind of planning would preserve academic freedom. The pathos comes, in this argument, when we remember that UNC officers had refused to do such planning from 1973 through 1980. Chapter Five expands on this paradox, which explains why program consolidation had been the biggest bone of OCR–UNC contention since 1977.

Dr. Donald Smith, at one time President of the University of Wisconsin, devoted much of his testimony as an expert witness for UNC to a critique of degree program consolidation. His major position was that

> the principal factor in student choice is the perception of the student of the fitness of the institution for his or her particular assumptions about the kinds of institutions he wants to attend, the kinds of demands he's ready to face. . . . Why is it that students . . . show up at the University of Wisconsin, Madison, which [sic] would not be required by the *de facto* admission requirements there. Well, it is a perception on the part of strong students . . . that this is an extremely demanding institution, academically.[13]

Dr. Smith explained that the University of Wisconsin at Madison does not uphold stringent admissions standards, yet it "composes itself" of high achievers. What he argues, although we see it as falling far short of the student choice process, is what made us recommend degree program consolidation! When white students in North Carolina can see that the TBIs are becoming what Smith calls "the kinds of institutions they want to attend," they will apply and enroll in increasing numbers. If Smith's reasoning is sound even in part, it illuminates the fact that the determinants of student choice at black colleges can no longer be limited to race and location of campus. One of the few ways to transform that historically limiting mission is to place degree programs there that change the academic options directly.

Desegregation of Graduate and Professional Students

It is easier by far to accomplish desegregation of graduate and professional students. Here we assumed a change from 12 percent black in 1979 to 20 percent black in 1990 (see Table A–11). This rise would itself reflect important progress in desegregation by bringing the graduate enrollments of blacks up to the undergraduate proportions of the previous decade. In modeling distributions, we took geographic locations and degree programs into account as well.

The first policy change required in order to achieve the goal would be to intensify recruitment of blacks at each major graduate campus by two to three times the current rates. Chapel Hill hosted 140 black students in the medical and other professional schools in 1979, for example. It would have to raise that base to 340 by 1990. East Carolina, the new medical school, enrolled 5 blacks in 1978, when its first entering class was small. As its first year enrollments reach 200 by 1985, 40 to 50 entrants should be black.

White student recruitment at the TBIs can parallel this intensification. Central has 225 whites now and, given its expanding law and library science schools, it could easily reach a white enrollment of 805 by 1990—easily, that is, if a policy commitment existed.

Only A&T needs very intensive changes in graduate programs. Its engineering and graduate education programs now host 139 whites. To reach our hypothetical goal of 320 by 1990, however, something more *magnetic* would have to be introduced. Our study of programs led us to recommend placing all graduate study in applied environmental science and engineering at A&T. North Carolina State nearby would continue its major programs in environmental studies, but the *applied* programs would be concentrated at A&T, linking that campus with the huge R&D center of the U.S. Environmental Protection Agency inside the adjacent Research Triangle.

Desegregation of Faculty

We also designed a redistributive model for UNC faculty desegregation (see Table A–12). Current base numbers were changed in order to anticipate faculty growth due to enrollment increases, fitted to each campus to preserve current teacher-student ratios. Using UNC's own demographic estimates, full-time faculty will grow from 6,532 in 1979 to 6,810 in 1990. Here, we used an overall goal of 15 percent black because the current proportion of 11 percent changed by only .2 percent in a five-year period, when 20 new white professors were hired for every one black professor, and because we doubt that a 20 percent standard could be achieved in the national marketplace.

In our model, then, UNC would have 1,042 black faculty in 1990, an increase of 336 over 1979. It would at the same time raise the number of white faculty at the TBIs from 252 to 475. To increase the availability of black faculty, we proposed a mutual assistance consortium among the main graduate centers, headquartered at Chapel

Hill, to build up the number of black Ph.D.s in such fields as the sciences and engineering.

Further analysis showed us that a policy of recruiting three to five black professors per year, depending on turnover, at each TWI, combined with a policy of white hiring for new growth and for replacements at TBIs, would achieve the goals.

Desegregation of Administrative Staff

Administrative desegregation would be harder to achieve than faculty desegregation, we found, yet it is equally feasible (see Table A–13). In 1979, 93 percent of all black administrators were at the five TBIs. In 1977 and 1978, expansionary years for UNC, some 149 new administrators were hired, 145 of them white; the number of blacks shrank from 231 in 1975 to 195 in 1979. Our goal was an increase in the proportion of black administrative staff from 16 to 20 percent by 1990.

Analysis showed that desegregation of administrators could be achieved solely by filling vacancies caused by annual turnover with cross-race appointees. We calculated the numbers of hiring opportunities on the one hand and the cross-race frequencies on the other. We found the opportunities would be ample and that an average of 2.4 whites per year at each TBI and two blacks per year at each TWI would result in desegregation.

THE DEBATE

Objections to our models for desegregating were not directed at their statistical assumptions or procedures. They were instead aimed at the very notion of policy changes that would be racially based rather than racially neutral. Graduate and professional students, said attorney Levin for UNC, are never "recruited," as we alleged; they apply and are "selectively admitted on the basis of merit." Faculty are sought by faculty search committees, and administrators are appointed after a screening for qualifications and leadership abilities. Our proposals were regarded as outrageously intrusive approaches exceeding even the already burdensome constraints of affirmative action guidelines.

Our view is that a century of racially based policies cannot be undone without unequivocal remedial action. This is not to neglect sources of progress already visible in the UNC system. Chapel Hill medical school has made strides on its own and its student body is probably the most completely desegregated at any medical school in the United States. Central's law school is drawing whites and will continue to do so. UNC already offers a few doctoral scholarships for current faculty, and this effort has produced ten Ph.D.s for black professors and a few for whites as well. For all of this, UNC has not put into place a single systemwide desegregative policy capable of redistributing students, faculty or administrators to levels even approximating our goals.

The difference between UNC's plans and our models is extreme because UNC's plans work against desegregation objectives. Those plans show that cross-race *eligibility* is universal, consistent with the end of *de jure* segregation in 1957. They show some small investments in financial aid for cross-race student enrollments, at least up to a million dollars a year. They show outreach for black students in some degree programs on some white campuses. Above all, they show that since *Adams* in 1973, movement of black students into some of the TWIs has been going on and will continue.

Beyond this, UNC had no plans other than to expand duplicative degree programs on TBI campuses. It had no racially oriented policies or aims that went beyond accepting the changes resulting from these early 1973 modifications. Our models, in stark contrast, set desegregation goals and enable UNC to plan to meet them. The actions to take would *have* to change the conventions of governance and campus autonomy. If taken, said UNC's attorneys and experts, UNC itself would be changed procedurally and academically as a result. We agree, and we believe that nothing less will eliminate the remains of a caste system.

Very divergent ideas about higher education underlie our thinking and that of those who spoke for UNC. The divergence is at base as old (or as new) as the question of who shall go to Oxford University. One of the many great contributions made to thinking about the issue by the revival of the Fourteenth Amendment and its further expression in court orders and statutes has been the continual clarification and redefinition of educational purposes, function, and design. That colleges should be open to a vast range of students and that those students will differ from those who went before have been transformative ideas, not only for the selection of students but also for programs of study, academic policies, and teaching methods themselves.

Since 1920, the American public high school has evolved raggedly and uncertainly from a place reserved for the most "deserving" and "promising" students—with major resources devoted to preparation of the college-bound few—toward a free, inclusive place of many options, with something of educational value for everyone. Since 1946, colleges in America have been following a similar evolutionary spiral. They are still much more differentiated and stratified than are high schools, to be sure; some campuses are much more inclusive as well as programmatically ecclectic than others. What is more, the pressure on colleges to remain or become highly selective is very great. Nevertheless, each year, the broadening out, the opening up, and the diversification of services continues to increase, but at rates that are exceedingly slow for blacks.

One of the many factors that tend to impede this evolutionary process is the need, especially within state-funded systems, to wear a mask when facing the public. The mask presents campuses as on some sort of a par, since they are all part of the system. This mask asserts that the colleges differ only in degree program offerings. The face behind the mask however, is competitive; it emphasizes sharp competition for prestige, resources, and self-determination. The public catches glimmers of what the deeper differences are, but in general, popular interest is limited to athletic prowess, the flagship campuses, and news coverage of nearby schools. Legislative support hinges mainly on liaison with the system's headquarters and with local advocates for particular benefactions.

Under these circumstances, the reputation of each campus builds up gradually over time and the resulting *status quo* comes to seem precious because it does not rest on public accountability for public services rendered but on images of familiarity and generalized esteem. The inputs—who enrolls, who gets the high school football stars, who recruits famous professors—become the story material that feeds the images, and the outputs—championship teams or high employability for graduates—obscure teaching and learning themselves. Preserving the imagery of campuses, cultivating their identifiability, as it were, often becomes the means for building fiscal security.

For UNC, the OCR approach, expressed through the Revised Criteria and our testimony, threatened not only the hegemony but also the institutional continuities of many UNC campuses. Above all, for instance, UNC worried that Chapel Hill would be degraded. Its doors might be opened to students of lower ability. Precious faculty resources would be given over to remedial services. Its flagship status would be jeopardized, warned Levin.

These worries were belied in the later testimony of Collin J. Rustin, Assistant Director of Admissions for Chapel Hill, on April 9, 1981. He explained the vigorous, enthusiastic, and increasingly effective work of his office to *recruit* black undergraduates. This effort coincides with the equally rigorous recruitment of other student subgroups, Rustin said, such as performing artists and athletes.

When Chapel Hill finishes its elaborate annual outreach and recruitment campaigns, its entering freshmen earn an average combined SAT score of about 1150. That is the highest mean for any UNC campus but it is 200 points below the nation's most selective colleges, from Harvard to Stanford University.

Levin and others also worried aloud about damaging the delicate continuities of the TBIs. As the highest-ranking black administrator in UNC, Vice President Lloyd Hackley put the concern this way:

> Students choose institutions because of certain ideas, attitudes they have about a particular institution, and how they'll fit in . . . The average student attending the TBI has scored lower on . . . the SAT . . . they . . . come from secondary schools that did not prepare them for college life . . . Students choose programs at the outset in which they feel they can succeed . . . Black kids think about higher education, they think about going to TBIs . . . They are now considered by black people as their institutions. That's where they want to go to school.[14]

Hackley said he feared that if TBIs became desegregated, fewer blacks who think of them now as "their own" would want to go to college. In contrast to his view, Alexander Astin's most recent survey of 187,000 entering freshmen in 1980 found that 51 percent said they chose their college "because it had a good academic reputation." Another 27 percent said they made their choice because their college "offers a special program of study."[15]

Hackley also said, speaking of a visit to Winston-Salem University, that "a number of students told me and showed evidence that they could have gone anywhere inside the system or even outside but they had chosen a TBI because they wanted to go there. 'We like this institution.' 'My father went to this institution.' 'My brother went.' 'We like this school.' 'We want to be here.' "

Aside from the fact that it would have been hard for fathers to attend Winston-Salem because it was a girl's college until 1973, Hackley neglected Astin's survey finding that 47 percent of the 1980 freshmen had fathers who never went to college. *Mass* access means that every year in America, some 50,000 prospective freshmen make decisions without benefit of what Hackley and others call family historical connections and advance feelings of "comfortableness."

During and after desegregation, the UNC campuses would change, and with this, the reasons for choosing one campus over another would change. Hackley is right, however, in thinking that *some* black students would not apply because of the change. As community college and technical institutes have expanded and improved in North Carolina, as in other states, four-year colleges dependent on students of lesser ability have been hard pressed to compete.

Many of the students Hackley worries about would enter those alternative schools instead, and many of them would transfer as juniors into UNC degree programs of their choosing later on.

In Conclusion

Chapter Three will explore program differences and admissions practices in detail. Here, we close with the point that this book is really about differing visions of what colleges exist to do in a mass society. Our notion is that the public ones exist to provide access to and assistance with participation in higher learning, and that they do this at the expense and in the service of *all* who seek to enter and to study with seriousness of intellectual purpose.

We make no case against what Dr. Robben Fleming, former President of the University of Michigan and an expert witness for UNC, called a "kind of pecking order even within a system." He explained that some students seek prestige and bigness while others want a liberal arts program from a reputable smaller campus. We do make a case against a pecking order, however, which *deprives* some campuses of reputational adequacy and which isolates some students by race.

As the May 5, 1981 issue of *The Chronicle of Higher Education* reported, there is a nationwide change in undergraduate enrollments taking place now, coming from a dramatic upsurge in students over twenty-five years old on four-year campuses. Outreach toward older students is having a large, measurable effect. This and related changes led the Ford Foundation Commission on the Higher Education of Minorities to call, early in 1982, for a "value added" approach to admission, in which students would be evaluated "on the basis of their potential for learning and growth rather than their relative standing on tests and grades."[16]

Our next chapter explores some of the many ways in which some UNC *TWIs* have begun to attract and host students in ways fitted to their needs, interests, and learning potential. From the UNC point of view, their TBIs had accomplished just this ideal long ago by concentrating on educationally disadvantaged black students. The tragic flaw in this argument is that the ideal is *not* to commit whole universities to a singular social aim, but rather to open up and diversify opportunities on many campuses for a great variety of learners. Consolidation of degree programs is but an interim device for balancing the equities on the way toward this end.

What is owed a university student besides admission if qualified, a setting in which to learn, and a diploma upon completion of formal requirements? OCR moved to enforce compliance with Title VI, but its case at first did not confront the *many* levels of meaning inherent in that Title. Morgan and associates mustered a defense which challenged those many levels. To comply, said Levin, would be to challenge and alter the foundations of UNC. Governance, academic freedom, efficiency criteria for allocating monies, the pecking order of campuses, campus autonomy, and even the uniquenesses of the flagship, Chapel Hill, would have to change in deep ways, all because the slender stick of civil rights was to be poked under the grand rock of academic custom.

Our models for desegregating showed that desegregation can be accomplished over an eight-year period, but only if the state system's leadership is willing or is forced to commit to making *deep* changes in their current plans. Those changes would be both curricular and financial and would move UNC toward full equalization of its comparable campuses. Just how deep those moves would have to be is developed in the next two chapters.

NOTES

1. James S. Coleman, "Equality of Opportunity and Equality of Results," *Harvard Educational Review*, 43, Fall 1973, pp. 129–137.

2. A. Harry Passow, ed., *Opening Opportunities for Disadvantaged Learners*, Teachers College Press: New York, 1972, pp. 8–9.

3. Higher Education Research Institute, *Minorities in Higher Education; 1982 Summary Report*, 924 Westwood Blvd., Suite 835, Los Angeles, CA, 90024.

4. *New York Times*, February 7, 1982, p. 56, Col. 4.

5. OCR itself has used this definition in some instances, for example in the early stages of setting eligibility criteria for Emergency School Assistance grants. It is also used as part of the Racial Imbalance Act of Massachusetts.

6. *Milliken v. Bradley*, 1974, 418 U.S.717, 741n.19.

7. Charles V. Willie, *Sociology of Urban Education*, D.C. Heath Lexington Books: Lexington, MA., 1978.

8. Robert A. Dentler et al., *The Urban R's: Race Relations in Urban Education*, Praeger: New York, 1967.

9. Gregory Kannerstein, *A Comparative Study*. We were also told by southern black educators that North Carolina A&T had often been penalized during the 1930s and 1940s for the political organizing efforts of some of its black faculty, and during the 1960s A&T students were early activists in the civil rights movement of that decade. See Miles Wolff, *Lunch At the Five and*

Ten: The Greensboro Sit-ins—A Contemporary History, Stein and Day: New York, 1970.

10. Higher Education Research Institute, *Minorities in Higher Education.*

11. William Fuller, *Campus Facilities of the University of North Carolina,* Washington, DC: Office for Civil Rights, 1979.

12. Gregory A. Jackson, *Sociologic, Economic, and Policy Influences are College-going Decisions,* Institute for Research on Educational Finance and Governance, Stanford University, 1981. Also, Alexander W. Astin, *Four Critical Years,* Jossey Bass: San Francisco, 1977.

13. *Adams v. Califano,* D.D.C. Civ. A. No. 3095-70, p. 11,723.

14. Ibid., p. 13,154.

15. Alexander Astin, et al., *The American Freshman: National Norms for Fall 1980,* Graduate School of Education, UCLA, 1981.

16. Higher Education Research Institute, *Minorities in Higher Education.*

CHAPTER 3

The Separate and Unequal Curriculum

Once it became clear that the white and black campuses differed in students, faculties, administrators, and type and range of degrees granted, the question of differences in curriculum offerings arose. A key issue in educational segregation has always been the question of exactly which students are permitted to study and learn which material. A corollary issue is the question of which students are allowed access to which tier of quality in education. These are at base caste or class issues, which under conditions of segregation reflect fundamental notions about relations between very separate and hierarchically ordered black and white societies. As Dollard penetratingly observed, in the segregated society, blacks constitute a separate and inferior caste in the eyes of the white majority.[1] Although the black caste may have a class hierarchy paralleling that of the white caste, it is nonetheless definitively and permanently inferior. Hence, opportunities and behaviors for members of the black caste are overtly and covertly restricted, as both symbol and source of inferiority.

For instance, *de jure* segregation hardened white cultural assumptions about the subjects and areas of study "fit" for blacks who sought higher education. White Southern culture accepted and even approved of black elementary and secondary school teachers and principals for black schools, black clerical help and black businessmen to serve the black community, black ministers and church staff, a few "prosperous" black small farmers, and the occasional black professional. The black colleges of the South were traditionally limited to preparing blacks for these occupations, most particularly for that of educator. Hence, black campuses were historically little more than normal schools or teachers' colleges. This was true even of an ostensibly technical land grant school (like UNC's A&T), whose distinction might have been a few agricultural and engineering courses grafted onto its normal school trunk. Thus a university system that has failed to correct for past segregative practices shows strong echoes of this past in terms of which institutions are allowed to offer which courses.

After *Brown, de facto* segregation in lower education continued to play out these assumptions in more covert and subtle ways, repeatedly translating them into certain service delivery patterns throughout the South. Although *de jure* segregation was officially over in 1954, parallel, duplicative, inequitable, and racially separate educational services continued to proliferate throughout the growth era from the mid-1950s to the early 1970s. School districts constructed new buildings, dispersed students, and offered educational programs in patterns that encouraged rather than discouraged segregation and racial separatism. For example, two new high schools—one for the black end of town, one for the white—would be built, rather than a single consolidated school in the center of town. Or, even more likely, one or two new high schools would be built at the white end of town, and the old black school would be repaired or remodeled a bit. Black and white schools would then proceed to offer duplicative programs in certain areas—for example, vocational education. Innovative, especially attractive, or enriching new programs would generally be placed at the white school, while the black was held to a minimalist curriculum.

Because higher education—particularly a state higher education system that serves a largely state and regional student population—is no less reflective of its society than is lower education, it is reasonable to expect a university system that has failed to correct for past segregative practices to show a similar developmental pattern. For example, its TBIs will have continued through the three post-*Brown* decades with minimalist educational offerings. In contrast, during these boom years its TWIs will have blossomed with a proliferation of offerings that duplicate and compete with those at the TBIs, as well as a dazzling array of additional courses and programs.

De facto segregation has seen another, still more subtle continuation of segregative caste maintenance: the notions of student ability tracking and tiers of "quality" or "difficulty" in educational offerings. In its simplist form, this manifestation of the caste system assumes that minority students are less able learners than white students, and segregates the former into special classes or institutions fitted to their limitations. These classes and institutions then become—either by design or by reputation—inhabitants of the lower tier of quality or educational difficulty.

This issue of student ability is especially complex and insidious, for it quickly becomes confounded with questions of real individual differences and deprivations among learners. In lower education, this problem has been somewhat resolved through litigation, careful use of diagnostic and prescriptive testing of students, and compensatory educational programming within mainstream settings. However, in higher education, the issue is just beginning to surface, and it is further confounded with traditional, widely shared visions and myths of the university as a place only for the brightest and the best.

The problem in higher education is exacerbated by the widespread use and general misunderstanding of the Scholastic Aptitude Test (SAT). In lower education, there are myriad tests of both student ability and student achievement in use. In addition, the past twenty years have seen the development and widespread adoption of highly individualized, instructionally linked testing. In contrast, the SAT reigns virtually unchallenged as "the test" for higher education. Designed as an aid to college admissions, the SAT (for a variety of largely non-measurement reasons) has come to be seen—both popularly and in academic circles—as an unspoken but immutable measure of the "quality" of both students and institutions.

Given that minorities generally score lower on the SAT (as a consequence of prior deprivation) than do white students and given the complexities of the other issues involved, the power of this test to reinforce segregative notions of who is "able" to study what in what sort of college or university is immense. It would not be at all surprising, for instance, to discover the defenders of an uncorrected university system arguing for its integrity on the basis of "tested" or "proven" differences in students' ability as measured by the SAT: minimal (black) institutions for minimally able (black) students; "superior", enriched (white) institutions for (white) students able to do the work.

In sum then, we sought to describe the differences in curriculum between UNC's black and white campuses and to test these differences for indicia of segregative practices. Simply stated, our tests were three: Did the TBIs' curricula show strong echoes of their severely restricted *de jure* past? Did the more recent curriculum development patterns across TBIs and TWIs suggest the type of differential service delivery patterns characteristic of the *de facto* era? Did the UNC SAT scores support UNC's implicit argument that it was a tiered system based on student ability, with weaker and stronger students grouped appropriately at less rigorous and more rigorous institutions?

WHITE VERSUS BLACK CURRICULUM

Our Analyses

We tested our questions about curriculum by means of straightforward analyses of the course offerings at the TBIs and TWIs in the UNC system. We elected to concentrate on course offerings rather than degree programs as definitive indicia of curriculum for several reasons. First, courses are the *sine qua non* of an institution. Second, courses offer a more concrete level of data than do degree programs. Third, the picture at the program level is easily inflated, as the same course can and usually does show up repeatedly in several programs. Finally, the UNC institutions varied considerably in the degree to which they were able to format a sophisticated catalog at the program level. Some campus catalogs were elegant masterpieces in this regard; others were mundane at best. Analysis at the program level would have been weighted too heavily by such differences in self-presentation.

We obtained each institution's most current catalog as of late spring/summer of 1980, either from the institution itself or the microfilm files at Harvard's Gutman Library. We then reviewed each catalog, counting the courses listed and classifying them by major subject area. For comparative purposes, we arrayed the various institutions roughly by type and size.

A quick scan of the first few catalogs we obtained revealed substantial variation in the presentation of courses. To organize our recording of these variations, we developed several decision rules to guide our counts. Although these rules worked very well for the most part, two proved vulnerable to procedural challenge by UNC. The details of that challenge are discussed later; in essence, however, it led us to conduct a complete recount of over 16,500 courses in all fifteen catalogs. Both analyses led inescapably to the same conclusions. (See Appendix B, Tables B–1 and B–2, for a presentation of the decision rules used.)

Overall, we found the TBIs' academic offerings to be significantly underdeveloped in comparison with those at the TWIs. The latter generally dramatically outstripped the former in both breadth and depth of curriculum. In addition, the TBIs clearly showed vestiges, if not continuation, of segregative practice. While this pattern was not without exceptions, the overall trend was unmistakable. In fact, it was so strong that we could not imagine a set of counting rules that would mask it, short of adopting deliberate biases to disguise the effect—and inventing these would require considerable creativity!

The pattern became even more evident and poignant when we considered the dramatic growth and development enjoyed by certain TWIs during the past fifteen to twenty years. In particular, Greensboro, Wilmington, Western, Charlotte, Appalachian, and East Carolina have blossomed profusely—sometimes in direct competition with neighboring TBIs—with both traditional and especially attractive new courses and programs. In contrast, the TBIs, even in their more developed academic areas, have continued to bear the characteristic marks of their heritage as seriously limited normal schools designed to prepare blacks for a considerably restricted range of occupations. (Specifics of this general pattern are presented in Appendix B, Tables B–3 through B–7.)

For instance, in the area of *business and commerce*, the black campuses showed some healthy development (see Tables B–3 and B–4). In particular, Fayetteville and Central appeared to have considerable breadth and depth of offerings, and within both the general baccalaureate and comprehensive categories, the TBIs appeared generally able to compete favorably with the TWIs.

Beneath this good news, however, business and commerce course distributions in the UNC system reflected the heritage of the separate and unequal curriculum. First, the depth and breadth of the business and commerce development at the larger TWIs (Appalachian, Greensboro, East, State, and Chapel Hill) generally outstripped that at the TBIs (with the possible exception of Central).

This finding might have been understandable had it been confined to the two flagships, State and Chapel Hill, which have been well developed, prestigious schools for some time. However, when we considered that Appalachian, Greensboro, and East Carolina have grown most dramatically in the past ten to fifteen years, we were forced to question UNC's committment to eliminating the institutional duplication and competition that is rooted in past segregative practices. For example, Greensboro's offerings in business and commerce have been allowed and encouraged to develop within a few miles of A&T's.

The distribution of courses in business education, distributive education, and office administration was also illuminating. On the one hand, such courses were heavily concentrated at black institutions: 81 percent of such courses taught within the UNC system at general baccalaureate institutions were taught at TBIs, as were 68 percent of those taught at comprehensive campuses. On the other hand, such courses made up a significant proportion of the business and commerce offerings at the TBIs. In fact, they constituted 24 to 26 percent of the business and commerce offerings at all except one TBI, Elizabeth City. In contrast, only two of the five comprehensive or baccalaureate TWIs offered meaningful numbers of such courses, and they were in notably lesser proportion than was typical at the TBIs.

This pattern strongly suggested the segregative normal school heritage of the TBIs, echoing the time when higher education for blacks meant teacher training and little else. A more positive construction of the evidence would be that the concentration of business education offerings at the TBIs was a magnetic differentiation into this subspeciality. Unfortunately, competing or potentially competing courses manifest at certain TWIs lead us to discard this more positive interpretation. For instance, Appalachian and Western both offered business education courses sufficient to compete with Winston-Salem in the western half of the state, and Eastern vastly overshadowed Elizabeth City and Fayetteville in the eastern half. Similarly, Greensboro seemed quite able to compete with A&T in this subspeciality. The especially duplicative and directly competitive nature of the Greensboro/A&T situation was made even more apparent when UNC indirectly revealed that the A&T program had received accreditation, but the Greensboro program had not: why then had the Greensboro program been allowed to continue, or even to develop at all?[2]

The business and commerce offerings were illuminating in one additional and very important respect. The TBIs lagged substantially behind the TWIs in the area of business information systems. The special application of computer technology and management information systems to business and commerce is one of the most rapidly growing and high-demand fields in America. Consequently, courses aimed specifically at this field are very attractive to students. Among the smaller general baccalaureate campuses, the TWIs offered 61 percent of such courses; among the smaller comprehensive campuses, 75 percent (Table B–4).

The business and commerce curriculum patterns were echoed in education, the social sciences, the humanities, and the biological and physical sciences. Again and again the TBIs emerged as seriously underdeveloped in ways that strongly suggested both the segregated past and a less than equitable present.

For instance, *education* offerings were widely dispersed throughout the UNC system (Table B–4). Given that education is a rapidly declining field, this immediately suggested a need for some consolidation and an opportunity to devise nonduplicative and attractively differentiated speciality offerings across the various UNC campuses. Nonetheless, the few high-demand educational fields of the 1960s and 1970s—reading, speech pathology and audiology, special education, and early childhood education—were either underrepresented at the TBIs in comparison with the TWIs, or else were almost equally present at both types of schools.

For example, 67 percent of the special education courses taught at the smaller baccalaureate and comprehensive institutions were found at Pembroke, Wilmington, or Western. In fact, eight of the ten TWIs mounted this speciality, with seven of these providing at least five courses, and usually double or quadruple that number. In contrast, of the TBIs, only Winston-Salem and A&T showed five or more special education courses. With one exception (Elizabeth City), a similar pattern prevailed for speech pathology and audiology. The speech pathology and audiology offerings of any TWI mounting this speciality exceeded—and usually tripled—the offerings at the TBIs that provided this concentration.

In assessing the pattern in education offerings, it was especially illuminating to examine the recent growth of Pembroke, the TWI with a normal school heritage very similar to that of the TBIs. In three of the high-demand, modern educational specialties, Pembroke had come in the past decades to substantially outstrip the TBIs. In reading, Pembroke at least tripled the offerings of Winston-Salem, Fayetteville, and Central; it almost doubled A&T's; and it meaningfully exceeded Elizabeth City's. In special education, and early childhood education, Pembroke exceeded all but A&T (which it virtually equalled).

The *social sciences* presented a somewhat brighter picture (Table B–4), for five of the nine basic social science areas did not show any dramatic discrepancies between TBIs and TWIs. Although there was variance across black and white institutions in history, political science, psychology, criminal justice, social work, and sociology, the TBIs were generally comparatively well equipped with courses in these areas.

However, this was not the case for anthropology, economics, geography, and, surprisingly, home economics. For example, anthropology, which is generally considered a "rounding-out" offering in the undergraduate social sciences (especially given a good sociology offering), was sadly underdeveloped at all five TBIs. The only TWIs that offered few enough anthropology courses to be considered similarly underdeveloped were Asheville and Pembroke. Without ex-

ception, the other eight TWIs offered impressive depth in anthropology. This was even the case at State, which could offer a most
respectable fourteen courses in anthropology—this in spite of the
fact that agricultural and technical schools have not traditionally
stressed the social sciences. Its ostensibly analogous black campus,
A&T, had only two anthropology courses.

Economics, which is a high-demand field in modern America and
an essential support for a good business school, showed a similar
distribution. Of the smaller general baccalaureate schools, 57 percent
of the economics courses were found at TWIs. Pembroke exceeded
two of the TBIs in number of courses, and Asheville and Wilmington
could easily rival Fayetteville in extent of offerings. The point came
home when we remembered that Asheville had only very recently
broken out of its long tradition as a liberal arts school and begun to
offer business programs, that Pembroke has reached beyond its normal school heritage only in the past few years, and that Wilmington
is a comparatively young institution. At the comprehensive level,
Charlotte easily rivaled A&T in economics courses, and exceeded
Central. Again, it is worth remembering that Charlotte is comparatively a young campus. With the exception of Eastern, the remaining
TWIs far outstripped the general baccalaureate TBIs, and almost
equalled or surpassed Central.

In the *humanities* (Table B–5), A&T and State appeared quite comparable in architecture. And all five TBIs mounted fairly respectable
numbers of courses in the fine arts, with the two flagships, A&T and
Central, perhaps naturally offering the most breadth and depth in
this area. But even these two senior black institutions were outshone
in the fine arts among the smaller schools by little Pembroke and by
newly developed Western and Charlotte. Their offerings were overwhelmed by those of Greensboro, Eastern, and Chapel Hill. Even
the young Appalachian and the agricultural and technical State could
look A&T and Central in the eye.

More or less this same pattern prevailed for the remainder of the
humanities fields. Typically, A&T and Central mounted the greatest
breadth and depth of offerings. The other three TBIs tended to show
less breadth and depth of offerings than any of the TWIs, regardless
of the latter's size or developmental history. In fact, the TWIs' humanities offerings generally equalled or exceeded those at A&T and
Central, which then paled into insignificance beside the richness of
offerings at the larger TWIs. There were only two exceptions to this
general pattern. The first was the journalism offerings at both A&T
and Central, which meaningfully exceeded offerings elsewhere, except at East and Chapel Hill. (However, they did not approach
the depth of Chapel Hill's thirty-one courses.) The second was the

music offerings at the TBIs, which were notable at all five and were only matched among the five smaller TWIs by Pembroke and Wilmington.

The *biological and physical sciences* revealed some of the most glaring instances of TWI-TBI campus differences within the UNC system (Tables B–6 and B–7). For example, excluding the more limited subspecialities of agriculture and forestry from immediate consideration, it was quickly apparent that, among the smaller campuses, the TWIs could generally offer both more depth in biology per se and more depth across more subspecialities (e.g., biochemistry) than did the TBIs. The smaller general baccalaureate TWIs typically offered more *in toto* in the biological sciences than did the similar TBIs, even though it was the latter that were offering the nursing and medical technology programs. Among the smaller comprehensive campuses, the young Western and Charlotte were neck-and-neck with the senior A&T and Central. Finally, of the remaining TWIs, even Asheville, traditionally a liberal arts college, could mount more total offerings than the general baccalaureate TBIs, and the other four overwhelmed even A&T and Central.

Of particular interest was the comparison among neighboring Greensboro, A&T, and Winston-Salem. Greensboro competed well, in fact offering more depth in biology than any of the TBIs except A&T, which it essentially equalled. Since all three of these campuses offered nursing training, the potential for overdevelopment and for detrimental competition among them appeared substantial.

In the physical sciences, the TBIs compared fairly well in chemistry, mathematics, and physics. However, the TBIs were exceptionally weak in statistics, an important math subspeciality. Seventy percent of the TWIs offered statistics in notable depth, but the TBIs had very little to offer.

Unfortunately, comparisons in the other physical sciences were not as positive. For instance, the black campuses were significantly underdeveloped in the earth sciences and the environmental sciences and ecology, both important scientific fields for the energy industry. For example, in geology, 70 percent of the TWIs mounted respectable offerings. In contrast, only Elizabeth City could offer any serious depth in this field. Perhaps even more telling, A&T, a technical school, offered no geology, in comparison with State's glittering array of forty-two courses.

Even more disturbing were the engineering offerings, which, of course, were limited to A&T, Charlotte, and State. The comparisons are obvious from Table B–7, and we will not belabor them here. It is noteworthy, however, that A&T could not offer any civil engineering at all, was outstripped in electrical engineering by Charlotte, and was buried in comparison with State's awesome offerings. The numbers in the tables mask another aspect of A&T's engineering program, as reflected in the catalogs. The courses offered at A&T appear to be the ordinary array of engineering studies. In contrast, Charlotte's catalog suggests some very sophisticated and innovative ways of teaching and applying engineering (e.g., urban environment applications).

Finally, the spread of computer science offerings proved particularly telling. Computer science/"high tech" is of course the demand field of our times, and has been booming since the late 1960s and early 1970s. This reality was reflected in the UNC system by the fact that every TWI offered courses in computer science. Even Asheville, historically a liberal arts college, and Pembroke, historically a normal school, mounted a minimal offering of seven or eight courses in this field, and most of the TWIs offered two to four times as many. However, of the five TBIs, only Winston-Salem and Fayetteville exceeded the minimal TWI offering of seven courses. The two black flagship campuses, A&T and Central, offered virtually nothing in this critical field.

A&T and Central's shortfalls were particularly notable. These institutions are within easy reach of one of the most impressive computer installations in the entire nation, that of the Research Triangle area. In addition, North Carolina has a strong commitment as a state to "go high tech," and is making a major push to attract the industry. In fact, North Carolina has recently established the only state-sponsored, residential, science and mathematics high school in the nation, the North Carolina School for Science and Mathematics in Durham. The school's express purpose is to provide the state with a scientific and technological labor force to help usher in the high-tech era.[3] Against this backdrop, it was more than a little disturbing to find A&T and Central so lacking in scientific and technical fields.

The serious underdevelopment of the TBIs in the sciences was striking and seemed to sum up both the nature and significance of the TBI-TWI curriculum differences in general. These scientific fields are products of our modern age, and they have seen explosive growth since *Brown*. This growth has provided ample opportunity to redefine institutional heritages and recharge institutional futures. These opportunities have been ably seized for the TWIs in ways clearly unmatched for the TBIs. We can only conclude that this disparity indeed represents a failure to rectify segregative practices, whether *de jure* or *de facto*. The net effect is to seriously shortchange and dampen the curriculum and educational offerings of the TBIs, thereby restricting and dampening the educational opportunities of the students who attend these institutions.

The UNC Reaction

UNC never directly closed on the questions raised by our curriculum analysis. Rather, the UNC attorneys mounted an actuarial defense, attacking the validity of our technical assumptions and the accuracy of our basic course counts. It is impossible to ascertain whether or not this essentially procedural argument would have constituted UNC's main line of defense with regard to the curriculum questions, for, with the signing of the consent decree, the hearing ended before UNC presented its case-in-chief.

However, implicit in UNC's depositional and courtroom examinations of government witnesses, its exhibits and documents filed with the court, and its choice of witnesses and their depositional statements was what appeared to be a central pillar of UNC's main defense: a market model explanation of virtually every difference between TBIs and TWIs. While the procedural challenges to the validity of our curriculum analyses were significant (as discussed shortly), the market model defense was much more complex and subtle, and lay much closer to the heart of the case. As such, it potentially constituted a deep challenge to the *meaning* of any curriculum analysis we might do.

Hence, although we have already noted this defense argument in relation to distributions of students, faculty and administrators, it bears repeating and emphasizing here. When applied to our curriculum analyses, it clearly illuminates a nexus of UNC's case, which turned in part on a traditionalist vision of the university as a very selective institution for the higher education of the brightest and the best.

In essence, UNC argued both directly and by implication that *any* differences observed between TBIs and TWIs were natural, straightforward functions of similarity among students in peer group identification, and students' levels of achievement and ability. In the free market of the UNC system, students went, through self-selection, into those nearby constituent institutions where they felt most comfortable, particularly with regard to academic challenge (but with little or no consideration of specific offerings). This led very obviously to differences among the various campuses in faculty composition, degree programs, courses, and other features, as the institutions composed themselves to meet the demands of the students who clustered there.

The process was not in the least invidious, for it allowed everyone to seek his or her own level. The less able students would naturally cluster together at one campus, the brightest at another. The curriculum and degree program offerings at the campuses would naturally be different, since the less able students would neither be able to nor wish to pursue the same courses of study as the brightest students. The reverse would also be true, since the brighter students would not care to pursue the less challenging offerings designed for the less able. Further, any sort of course or program consolidation or magnetization would damage these natural orderings and throw the lower ability students into competition with the brighter group. This would be detrimental for everyone, but most particularly for the less able students. In fact, such action would probably mean the end of access to higher education for the lower ability students, since mixing of ability levels would inevitably lead to upgrading of all offerings on the mixed campuses. The less able students would then either not be able to keep up, would be discouraged from seeking admission, or would even actually be refused admission under new, higher standards.

During the pretrial discovery process of the depositions, it became clear that UNC was prepared to offer evidence (SAT scores of entering freshmen) to establish that the unifying ability distributions of its students quite circumstantially broke along racial lines. In other words, the lower ability students happened to be black and, due to similarity of peer group identification and achievement/ability levels, happened to cluster at the TBIs. Similarly, the higher ability students happened to be white and, again due to similarity of peer group identification and achievement/ability levels, happened to cluster at the TWIs. Curriculum and program offerings naturally differed across the two types of institutions, because each market segment of students needed and desired different things. And, consolidation or magnetization would actually work against equity for blacks since the less able black student would be thrown into detrimental competition with more able whites and would thus inevitably lose the educational race.

It was in fact the emergence of this defense theme that led us to join the issue of differences in student ability—or rather, SAT scores—as a part of our direct testimony. Certainly it is an issue that arises in curriculum analysis in general, and, as noted earlier, it has a long history in educational segregation problems in lower education. However, the particular danger in UNC's adoption of this line of defense was its subtlety and essential covertness. It seemed to us that there was a very real possibility that UNC would never fully and openly develop the argument, but rather would present only its vague outlines, thereby banking on its powerful intuitive appeal. Therefore, as discussed shortly, we chose to go directly to the issue and open it for argument.

While far less central than the market model argument, UNC's procedural challenge to the validity and reliability of our curriculum analyses was not inconsequential. In fact, had it ultimately succeeded, there would have been no need to mount the deeper challenge (with regard to curriculum). The procedural argument turned on two issues: Was a course count a valid approach to curriculum analysis? Had we accurately counted the courses in the various catalogs?

In challenging the basic validity of the course count method, UNC argued that there is much more to a complete curriculum assessment than counting courses. For instance, opportunities for special enrichment (or remediation), laboratory equipment, exchange programs, depth of sequences and "quality" of courses—as well as myriad other details—have to be taken into account for full understanding and explication of curricula.

Without doubt, carrying our analyses to these levels of detail would have refined and deepened our perceptions and honed our conclusions. Nevertheless, though we recognized and concurred fully with these broader UNC criticisms, we felt securely confident about the basic value and applicability of our analyses, for one fundamental fact was irrefutable: describing (that is, counting) the basic array of course offerings is the starting point of any sound curriculum analysis. Subsequent and deeper levels of assessment would no doubt refine the picture. However, the basic count reveals the foundation, framework, and roof of the curriculum, thereby displaying at least the gross outline of the academic house. UNC witnesses conceded this point under the government lawyers' questioning.

In challenging the accuracy of our course count, UNC took quick advantage of our failure to declare our counting rules in direct testimony and of our failure to compute error rates for the count. As mentioned earlier, we had developed a set of counting rules to deal with the substantial variation in catalog format and presentation (see Table B–1). For the most part, these rules worked very well. However, due to the sheer magnitude of the counting task, it became difficult to consistently apply the rule (#4) dealing with special content courses. Of greater importance was our decision (rule #5) sometimes to collapse biological and physical science courses under a main heading and sometimes to spread them into speciality headings.

In brief, UNC attempted to replicate our counts. Although UNC was not cognizant of our counting rules, its replications were for the most part quite consistent with our original counts. However, in some cases, most particularly in the physical and biological sciences, the replications were very different. It was largely from this difference that the UNC challenge to the accuracy of our counts derived its credibility and power.

In direct response to this challenge, which we planned to address in depth in our rebuttal, we undertook a complete recount of all the catalogs. For our recount, we also changed some of the major decision rules to address other criticisms that UNC had raised, thereby specifically testing their implication that our conclusions depended on the rules we had used and not on the data. (The recount rule changes and their impact on the data are given in Table B–2.) As noted earlier, the recount served to confirm our conclusions solidly.

Finally, we conducted some reliability checks to estimate better our error rate in counting. Given the complexity and sheer magnitude of the task, we naturally expected a certain degree of error, and the only issue for us was whether it was within acceptable social science standards. Our error rates were indeed quite good, ranging from 5 to 9 percent for the most part and never higher than 11 percent. This also served to support our conclusions, for even if one assumes that the errors always understate the strengths of the TBIs (not the case in fact), the curriculum differences generally far exceed these bounds.

In sum, had the case reached the rebuttal stage, we were very confident that we could successfully meet UNC's procedural challenges. However, the deeper defense argument was more problematic because of its complexity and subtlety. It turned in large part on the SAT scores, and on widespread misunderstandings about their meaning and proper application.

ABILITY AND ADMISSIONS

To reiterate, UNC was prepared to use the SAT scores of its entering freshmen to buttress two major defense arguments: (1) lower ability students voluntarily cluster within the system, and hence constituent institutions become specialized by student ability; (2) any curricular or programmatic consolidations or magnetizations involving the mixing of low- and high-ability students on the same campus would require such extremes of pedagogic adaptation as to be infeasible, and even if undertaken would be especially detrimental to lower ability (black) students. Therefore, insofar as ability is correlated with race, any observed racial differences among campuses are either incidental or determined by the market, as are any observed curriculum differences. Further, any attempts to upset this natural balance would be destructive, both individually and institutionally, and would work against increasing access for minorities.

Our counterargument took two separate thrusts. First, we raised some basic points about the measurement characteristics of the SAT. These served to challenge UNC's fundamental reliance on these scores as sweeping measures of student ability. Second, we examined the actual SAT score distributions across UNC's various campuses. This served to challenge UNC's more empirical presentation of the scores as supportive of its contentions about "natural" ability groupings of students and the potentially negative consequences of mixing students of varying ability.

Our Analyses

In terms of measurement issues, we sought to introduce four basic points about the SAT and its proper use. These points presented— from a very conservative perspective—some of the limitations of the SAT. Point number one was simply that the SAT is properly a supplemental device to assist in college admissions decision making. As such, it is designed to be coupled with other information, such as high school grades, recommendations, participation in extracurricular activities, and so forth. This usage is promulgated by the SAT designers and owners, the Education Testing Service (ETS), and is widely (if not universally) accepted even by select colleges and universities.[4]

Point number two was equally simple: the SAT is supplemental because it has inherent limitations as a predictor of success in college. It measures learned skills, not innate, unchanging abilities. As ETS states:

> A common misconception is that these tests somehow measure innate, unchanging abilities. In fact, they measure learned skills. They are described as aptitude tests because they are not tied to a particular course of study, curriculum or program, and because they are typically used to assess students' relative abilities to perform well in future academic work. They measure intellectual skills that students are expected to have developed through both school and non-school experiences, apart from the particular courses of study they may have pursued . . . the tests measure particular, defined skills that have a bearing on future academic performance . . . inferences about these skills cannot be made with any certainty.

and

It [SAT] measures intellectual skills learned through both
formal and informal educational experiences, skills that are exercised and further developed through application to school work
in a wide variety of academic subjects and through experiences
outside of school.[5]

The recent debate about the SAT's susceptibility to coaching further emphasizes this point. While much controversy abounds over
just what type and quantity of coaching or remedial instruction is
required to produce score gains, even ETS has recognized the possibility of gains through special instruction. Other educators and
researchers have reported some very dramatic student improvements
as a result of directed instruction.[6]

Point number three was that the SAT, even in conjunction with
high school grades, generally accounts for only a small portion of
variance in first-year freshmen's grades, again according to ETS's
own materials.[7] Certainly the ETS estimates of variance accounted
for can be criticized as either too high or too low, depending upon
one's statistical perspective.[8] In any case, however, the SAT by no
means accounts for even a major portion of the variance in first-year
freshmen's grades.

Point number four was that the SAT is typically used to predict
only one aspect of college students' performance—first-year grade
point averages. This can hardly be defined as conclusive success in
college. Studies of the SAT's relationship to more meaningful criteria
of success—for example, senior grade point averages, transfer rates,
dropout rates, cumulative grade point averages across the entire four
years of college, grades in particular courses or programs of study,
graduation rates, employability rates, professional certification rates,
and entry into professional or graduate training—are conspicuously
absent from the literature. And for the latter criteria, the SAT is not
even considered in practice. Employers do not look at SAT scores
when they screen applicants. Graduate and professional schools require other tests (tests of learning in the undergraduate years), and
rate undergraduate performance very highly.

Hence, the SAT's reputation rests almost entirely upon its relationship to student performance in the freshmen year. It is a truism
that even the most able students often experience a performance
slump in their first (or even second) year as they wrestle with the
social and psychological adjustments required by the shift from life
at home as high school seniors to life as freshmen in residence on a
college campus. In fact, many graduate and professional schools

(including the most select) very often weight student performance in the junior and senior years much more heavily than that in the freshman and sophomore years in their admissions algorithms.

Even those professionals who specifically study college students' success do not appear to view the SAT as a predictor variable of major interest, or freshman grades as an outcome of particular importance. A review of 460 articles from 1975 to 1980 revealed a myriad of predictors and outcome measures. The latter included, in order of frequency: cumulative grade point averages, course completion and graduation rates, particular course grades, performance on the instructor's exams, performance on specific learning tasks, various standardized tests, end-of-term grade point average, and courses or programs chosen. The first two measures were by far the most frequently used. Predictors were of three main types: (1) educational process factors (used in about 43 percent of the studies); (2) social/psychological factors (used in about 39 percent); and (3) demographic factors (used in about 18 percent). Certainly SAT scores and freshman grades are as readily obtainable as most of the measures used in this large body of research. Yet, they are conspicuous by their absence.

Even more important, this research clearly shows that many, many factors affect students' performance and college success to significant degree. For instance, educational process factors were positively related to success in 65 percent of the studies in which they were used; social/psychological factors, in 67 percent.

Finally, this research also speaks to the fundamental purposes of higher education: to teach and educate. In debates about entry-level ability or ability as measured by the SAT, this purpose is often obscured. Colleges and universities are not merely gathering places for students of like SAT scores. Rather, institutions of higher education without question have and exercise options—both through their larger governance and through their individual instructors—to control and change their educational services to meet the needs of their students. Instructors can and do manipulate teaching style, course format and structure, classroom environment, and so forth. Universities can and do manipulate the provision of counseling, living environments, extracurricular activities and financial aid and employment opportunities.

Put in perspective then, the SAT must be viewed as a limited and supplemental admissions device, which tests particular learned skills that have some "bearing on future academic performance [but about which] inferences . . . cannot be made with any certainty"; which is susceptible to coaching or developmental instruction; which accounts for a very modest portion of variance in freshman grades; and which has not been widely tested against other, more meaningful measures of college success. In addition, the SAT must be viewed in the context of a large body of research literature that establishes the overarching importance of many other predictors and definitions of success in college—including educational process features and cumulative student performance.

This more accurate view of the purposes, proper usage, and inescapable limitations of the SAT was in itself sufficient to call into serious question the validity of UNC's arguments. If the SAT is at best a weak and very limited predictor of success in college, SAT scores cannot be considered to be conclusive or even central measures of student ability. What then does it mean to observe score variations across UNC campuses? Is the variation a function of natural self-selection by students on some other measure or perception of ability? Or is it a function of race and segregative practices, masked by the fact that blacks—as a function of generations of social, economic, and educational deprivation—tend to score lower than whites on standardized tests in general, including the SAT? Further, given the limitations of the SAT, the contention that mixing students with different scores on the same campus is infeasible and potentially detrimental falls away.[9]

Still, UNC's arguments warranted tests against the data itself. This proved to be very illuminating. The SAT data revealed first of all that UNC, as a system, serves a student population with low to moderate SAT scores. It is not a highly selective system. As Table B–8 shows, with the exception of the math scores at the doctorate-granting TWIs, the UNC entering freshmen's scores are skewed towards the lower intervals (200–499). When the scores are broken into smaller intervals, as in Table B–9, this conclusion does not change. It is refined in that, for the most part, the entering freshmen score between 300 and 499, in the second- and third-lowest intervals.

Second, Tables B–8 and B–9 show that although this skewing varies by type of institution, all types of institutions do host all types of students, even, for the most part, those in the very highest and very lowest intervals. Certainly at the TBIs a notably larger portion of the entering freshman class scores in the very lowest interval. However, this must not obscure the fact that some of the entering freshmen at the TWIs also score in this range, as well as in the next lowest interval (300–399). Similarly, the TBIs have some freshmen who score in the highest intervals, although these do not constitute as large a proportion of their entering classes as they do at the TWIs.

The central fact that all types of UNC institutions host all types of students is also evidenced by the institutional score averages (Table

B–10). Although there are indeed mean score differences among the constituent institutions, these differences are a function of racial composition. Across the board, the black students' average scores tend to be lower than the white students' averages. (The two distributions do overlap considerably, however.) Hence, the greater the concentration of black students, the lower the institution's average score tends to be. This should not, however, obscure a critical central reality: low-scoring blacks and whites are to be found at every UNC campus, as are higher-scoring blacks and whites. (And, low-scoring blacks and whites apply to UNC in substantial proportion, as shown by Table B–11.)

Third, all types of UNC institutions showed a notable similarity in scores for what might be called their "core" bodies of entering freshmen, that is, the largest portion of their classes. As Table B–12 shows, with one exception (again the doctoral TWIs' math performance), the majority of entering freshmen in all types of UNC institutions score in the 300–499 interval on the SAT.

When the wide variances in institutional size are considered, these percentage distributions and averages are seen to be somewhat misleading. For instance, the three TWI doctoral campuses collectively hosted over 30,000 students, whereas all five TBI campuses hosted about 13,000. Indeed, as Table B–13 shows, the TWIs actually host larger numbers of low-scoring freshmen than do the TBIs. In fact, in some of the lower score intervals (e.g., 300–399 verbal), the TWIs hosted almost four times as many students as did the TBIs.

In sum, our analyses of UNC's scores also threw their arguments into serious question. The SAT data clearly showed that the UNC system as a whole—including its flagships—was simply not a highly selective or rigorously tiered system. UNC admits large numbers and proportions of freshmen scoring in the low and lowest SAT categories, and distributes them across *all* of its constituent institutions. This plus the observation that average institutional differences are a function of racial composition, clearly counters the notion that students cluster by ability.

These empirical facts also strongly counter the contention that dire pedagogic consequences would follow certain desegregative remedies (e.g., program consolidation). The UNC is already serving a low to moderate ability population and hence is already adapted. Further, students of varying abilities are already mixed at each of the constituent institutions. Those who scored high on the SAT go to school with those who scored low on the SAT every day, and all are apparently accommodated.

For instance, the fifteen catalogs were rich with descriptions not only of honors and enrichment programs, but also of support services for academically troubled students or those with potential in this direction. These ran the gamut from special study programs and courses to laboratories, compensatory and remedial classes, tutorials, counseling, workshops, and advisement opportunities. Their substantive content included math and developmental reading, language arts, writing, comunication skills, history, science, English and study skills, to name but a few. Even the three flagship campuses—Chapel Hill, State, and Greensboro—provide extensive support. In addition, the catalogs painted a picture of considerable leniency with regard to academic suspension and probation options. UNC students are typically given very generous opportunities to "make good" by repeating failed courses, often several times; electing pass/fail options; auditing courses before taking them for credit; and seeking tutoring and counseling after they find themselves in difficulty as well as before.

Clearly then, the observed institutional differences between TBIs and TWIs in course offerings and programs are not a function of differences in students' ability so much as past segregative practices. The echo of the old, segregated normal school that clings to the curriculum of the TBIs is not a special pedagogic adaptation for students in need of compensatory and developmental support. Such students are found everywhere in the UNC system, and the curriculum offerings of the TWIs that host them are considerably deeper and richer than those of the TBIs.

The UNC Reaction

As had been the case in our analyses of UNC curricula, UNC never directly closed with our arguments concerning admissions and students' ability. However, it was clear from the UNC attorney's challenges to Baltzell's testimony in this area that we had indeed struck a nerve. These challenges also made it possible to identify the likely shape of UNC's defense on these issues, had the consent decree not halted the hearing.

From the beginning, Baltzell's testimony on the SAT issues drew vigorous and continual challenges from the UNC table. She was first greeted with a sustained *voir dire* challenge when she introduced the measurement issues.[10] After this was overruled, she was interrupted repeatedly in her exposition of the measurement points by UNC's entry of objections and motions to have the testimony struck on the grounds of irrelevance. Finally, when she moved into her testimony on the SAT score data, she encountered repeated objections as to the accuracy and acceptability of her figures (all of which were overruled). In fact, no other aspect of Baltzell's testimony was challenged as heavily.

The main thrust of the UNC objections went to the question of how the SAT score distributions should be interpreted. For example, UNC viewed the distributions of institutional SAT means as illustrations of the extent to which campuses differed in average student ability: the TBIs had less able students than did the TWIs. Similarly, UNC viewed the distributions of SAT scores by interval as illustrations of campus specialization. The TBIs' student bodies tended to include larger percentages of the lowest scorers than did the TWIs': the TBIs specialized in low-ability students. It appeared that UNC would continue to stress these interpretations as the proofs of their two basic arguments.

As our analyses of the SAT data (and presentation of the measurement issues) showed, these interpretations are superficial and misleading at best. Nevertheless, in pursuing these arguments, UNC had two almost universally held biases working in its favor. First, on the empirical level, although ours was the deeper and more sophisticated treatment of the scores, UNC's approach was so obvious and intuitively attractive as to almost beg the question.

Second, on the deeper, conceptual level, we were certainly challenging widespread common-sense notions about just what test scores mean, and presenting a more accurate picture of the strengths and weaknesses of the SAT. But, for numerous reasons, almost all of us are reluctant to relinquish the myth of the test score as capturing the essence of ability and merit. If nothing else, we look to the test score as a means for simplifying complex and pressured decisions and assessments. The SAT (along with professional and graduate exams) is particularly sacred in this regard, for it has been promulgated as the arbiter of college entry and a central measure of American educational quality for twenty years. Consequently, though college admissions officers and test and measurement specialists may fully appreciate the limitations as well as the strengths of the SAT, the widespread notion of its power to reflect both student ability and educational and institutional quality remains deeply ingrained. By simply saying nothing about the measurement issues, UNC played directly to this popular bias, and the approach was once again so obvious and intuitively attractive as to almost beg the question.

In sum, the UNC reaction to our SAT analyses was very similar to the reaction to the curriculum analyses in two fundamental respects. First, challenges to the basic worth and validity of the analyses were vigorously mounted by the UNC attorneys. Second, and more importantly, UNC looked at the data in a different way and found a different meaning. To UNC, the SAT scores proved the existence of "natural" campus specialization according to student ability. To us, the same scores proved just the opposite.

In Conclusion

In the final analysis, the issues in this case reached to the very heart
of racial equity and the purposes of higher education in America.
Our analyses of the issues of both curriculum and student ability
revealed profound disparities between black and white institutions
that were not justifiable on the grounds of campus specializations
by student ability levels. Further, our work established that academic
program remedies were neither infeasible, unnecessary, nor potentially detrimental. UNC took an almost completely opposite stance,
arguing chiefly that the curriculum differences were the function of
a free market system wherein students naturally clustered by ability
(and other characteristics), thereby giving rise to self-designed campus differences. Further, any interference with this free market would
upset the natural balances to the serious detriment of both students
and institutions.

Underlying these two opposing positions were two very different views of what the modern American university is all about. We
led from a vision of the university as a richly diversified educational
environment, accessible and welcoming to students of widely varying
abilities, interests, and backgrounds, well able to accomodate to differing student needs and at the same time fully capable of meeting
deep and necessarily proactive responsibilities for racial equity. UNC
led from a much more limited view of the university as an elite,
selective institution in the European tradition, intended for the higher
education of the brightest and the best. In this vision, racial equity
considerations become at best a distraction, at worse a seriously damaging and diluting force.

These two positions deeply reflect both the myth and the reality
that characterize higher education in America today. On the one
hand, the UNC stance represents a widely held and very powerful
vision about the meaning and purpose of the university experience.
Ironically, this vision is realized by only a few of the most selective
and prestigious institutions in the nation (for instance, Harvard), and
then only partially. Yet, almost everyone who has attended or applied
to attend college internalizes and participates to some degree in this
vision.

On the other hand, our position represents the reality of higher
education in America. It is not highly selective. It is not only for the
brightest and the best. Most of the nation's colleges and universities—including those most wrapped in the reputational cloak of selectivity and quality—admit and effectively serve students of widely
diverse backgrounds and abilities. In fact, many deliberately compose
themselves in this way, for the experience of diversity is generally

regarded as educationally enriching and essential. Ironically, this is unquestioningly true of the UNC system, where every campus, including the flagships, hosts students of every description, and which as a system serves students of low to moderate ability.

The conflict between the myth and the reality is dramatically sharpened by the racial equity question, for this issue forces both the underlying myth and the empirical reality into sharp consciousness and open debate. Subtly racist notions about the intellectual and academic abilities of minority students and segregative traditions that restrict areas of study for minorities intersect dramatically and profoundly with the mythical vision of the university as an elite, selective institution. Hence, any contest about racial equity in higher education becomes immediately entangled with questions about the most fundamental nature and purpose of the university. In essence, those who judge and participate in such contests are forced to chose one vision or the other.

We cannot know whether our stance for reality and racial equity in higher education would have won out or not, since the hearing never went to judgment. Ironically, however, two prestigious commissions have recently issued reports and policy statements that support many elements of our position. After a three-year study, the Ford Foundation's Commission on the Higher Education of Minorities has called for changes in the ways colleges and universities select, admit, and teach minorities. The Commission calls on colleges "to adopt a 'value added' system, in which students would be admitted and evaluated on the basis of their potential for learning and growth rather than their relative standing on tests and grades."[11] On the selection and admissions side of this model, the Commission recognizes the limitations of norm-referenced standardized tests such as the SAT, and urges that these devices be used diagnostically rather than just in a traditional, predictive admissions algorithm. On the pedagogical side, the Commission urges that student evaluation be switched from the norm-referenced to the criterion-referenced model, that academic and personal support services be increased, that the number of minority faculty and administrators be increased, and that the world of higher education be made generally more hospitable to minorities.

Following on the heels of the Commission, the National Academy of Sciences' Committee on Ability Testing has just issued a major report that calls upon "all but the most selective colleges and universities" to reconsider the use of standardized tests like the SAT in admissions. The Committee bases its recommendations in part on the inherent limitations of such tests, and in part on "the special harm their improper use can cause minorities."[12]

That the benefits of these corrections would extend to all students seems obvious. Yet, illustrative of the pervasive power of the mythic vision of the university and its profound intersection with the racial equity question, the Ford Commission's central recommendation for a "value-added" approach was not received as beneficial by the higher education community. Rather, as Alexander Astin has noted recently, this recommendation has been widely misinterpreted as advocacy for "double standards" for minority students, as being "anti-test," and as a threat to academic standards.[13]

As Astin also comments, these misinterpretations arise from "the competitive and meritocratic values that permeate much of American society [and ultimately lead to subordination of] higher education's educational or value-added function to its screening and certification functions. That not only distorts the primary educational mission of higher education, but also unnecessarily limits opportunities in education by presupposing there will be 'winners' and 'losers.' "

In truth, the Ford Commission's central recommendation is a call to embrace the reality rather than the myth of the university in America, for the significantly greater benefit of all students and the larger society. Helped by the impetus of racial equity concerns, we may succeed in doing so.

NOTES

1.   Dollard, J. *Caste and Class in A Southern Town*, Yale Univeristy Press: New Haven, CT., 1937.

2.   This information was contained in the preparatory materials provided by UNC witness Eleanor Vernon. It is unclear whether Ms. Vernon was referring to the entire business and commerce offering at Greensboro, or to only business education, distributive education, and office administration offerings.

3.   Walton, S. "N.C. School of Science and Math: A Flare Burning Brightly." *Education Week* Vol. 1, No. 17, January 19, 1982.

4.   Educational Testing Service. *Test Use and Validity: A Response to Charges in the Nader/Mairi Report on ETS*. Educational Testing Service, Princeton, N.J. February, 1980.

5.   Ibid., p. 7–11.

6.   Slack, W.V. and Porter, D. "The Scholastic Aptitude Test: A Critical Appraisal." *Harvard Educational Reivew*, May 1980 Vol. 50, No. 2, 154–175; and Jackson, R. "The Scholastic Aptitude Test: A Response to Slack and Porter's 'Critical Appraisal.' " *Harvard Educational Review*, Vol. 50, No. 3, August, 1980, p. 383.

7.   Educational Testing Service, *Test Use and Validity*, p. 16.

8. Slack and Porter, "The Scholastic Aptitude Test."

9. This is not to imply that the SAT is unreflective of meaningful educational differences among students. Indeed, as both we and UNC witnesses recognized, the SAT is (or can be) pedagogically useful as a broad diagnostic device for aiding educational program designers in responding to student needs. It is quite reasonable to expect that students with very high scores (say 650–800) will be immediately responsive to extra stimulation, such as honors programs and accelerated or advanced courses of study. It is equally reasonable to assume that students with extremely low scores (say 250–300) will probably need some developmental support in the freshman (and possibly sophomore) year, such as study skills courses in certain areas, and perhaps lighter course loads per semester.

10. A *voir dire* challenge can be, among other things, an attempt to disqualify a witness from testifying on a topic on the grounds that she or he lacks the necessary expertise or has a personal stake in the issue.

11. Middleton, L. "Colleges Urged to Alter Tests, Grading for Benefit of Minority Group Students." *The Chronicle of Higher Education*, Vol. 23, No. 21, February 3, 1982, p. 1.

12. Biemiller, L. "Most Colleges Urged to Reconsider Use of Admissions Tests." *The Chronical of Higher Education*, February 10, 1982.

13. Astin, A.W. "Let's Try a 'Value Added' Approach To Testing." *The Chronicle of Higher Education*. July 28, 1982.

CHAPTER 4

The Economics of the Segregative University

The demographic and curricular patterns identified in the two previous chapters are the product not only of various admissions, staffing, and programmatic decisions by the UNC administration. They also are in part the result of the corresponding budgetary decisions made jointly by it and the North Carolina Legislature. Indeed, it is through the University's budget that all of its educational policies are ratified and implemented. It is reasonable, then, to ask to what extent the disparities identified in the two previous chapters translate into resource disparities. Or, alternatively, what do observable resource allocation patterns tell us about the magnitude of those disparities or about their source?

In earlier chapters, the question of resource allocation was occasionally alluded to or briefly noted. Here we look at it in detail. One reason for doing so is to show that the disparities identified in earlier chapters are real—that is, that UNC's allocation of resources across its constituent institutions reflects similar inequities. There are two other, and even more important reasons, however. First, analysis of resource allocations shows that these unequal outcomes are the direct product of UNC's budget decisions over the past fifteen years and that, without shifting of resources among campuses (e.g., through elimination of duplicate programs), they will not be reversed in the forseeable future. Second, such analysis rebutts the claims of the

UNC administration that the resource measures used here are inappropriate; that even if they are correct, they are of no educational consequence; that even if they are significant, they are really the result of factors beyond the University's control (i.e., UNC cannot be held liable for them); and that even if the University has some responsibility for current inequities, all of the solutions that would eliminate inequities within a short period of time would do more harm than good to both black and white students.

The analysis here is developed in three steps. The first section of this chapter presents a description of resource allocations at UNC and the evolution of those allocations over the past fifteen years; the focus of this narrative is on showing the reader just how the TBIs came to be "short-changed." The second section goes a step further to show that these inequities are directly linked to UNC's previous racial duality and that, because of current fiscal constraints on the University, it is only through reallocating existing resources that UNC can hope to eliminate disparities in the near future. Next, this evidence is reexamined in light of UNC's challenges to it. This reanalysis will show not only that the evidence withstands all of the challenges, but also that the challenges themselves imply a very cynical view on the part of the UNC administration concerning how the University should serve black students. The final section of the chapter sums up the conclusions to be drawn from analyzing this dimension of the North Carolina litigation and points out the major implications of those conclusions; a particular effort is made to show how the findings here might be generalized to the situation in other states.

How Shortchanging Works

Analysis of resource allocations at UNC represented the last piece in the government's overall case. The principal body of data on which the analysis was based had been introduced much earlier, as part of the government's general data base. For the analysis, these data were largely taken as given.[1] However, as the first step in the analysis (and the first part of the related testimony), the data were summarized into a set of nine statistical tables, which then became the principal focus of the remaining testimony. (These nine tables are presented as Appendix C.)

The tables were intended to serve three purposes: to condense the vast amount of data entered into evidence to a point where it could be digested by the court; to organize the data in a way that could provide a complete and coherent description of resource allocations at UNC; and to aggregate the data to a point which did not mask any serious disparities, but which did safeguard against the possibility that conclusions would be based on errors in the data or obscured by isolated, random deviations from the general allocation patterns. Although the methodology necessary to produce such tables was rather complex,[2] the salient features of the resulting products may be quickly summarized:

1. Data were reported for three time points; each "point" actually represented a two-year average:

    1964–66—the beginning of the system in its current form, with sixteen campuses, and the beginning of UNC's period of rapid expansion;

    1970–72—the mid-point of the study period and the time when the Board of Governors was created, the first *Adams* decision was rendered, and UNC's expansion slowed considerably; and

    1976–78—the last years for which data were then available.[3]

2. The figures reported represented averages for schools of like mission and racial identity. The fifteen campuses were collapsed into six groups for this purpose: general baccalaureate TBIs, general baccalaureate TWIs, comprehensive TBIs, comprehensive TWIs, small other TWIs, and large other TWIs.

3. Capital and operating expenditures were treated separately. The latter were divided into four categories (academic, support, plant and equipment, and other) to emphasize their relationship to the academic process.

4. Multiple measures of number of students served were used, in part to show how the choice of a particular measure affects the figures reported; however, the measure of "full-time equivalent students" was given the most attention, because of its general acceptance by recognized experts as most appropriate for assessing the comparability of educational resources and services.

Overall, the empirical measures represent an appropriate set of measures for evaluating the financial status of institutions of higher education and for comparing resource allocations across institutions.[4] Moreover, the data are highly consistent across sources, across institutions, and over time; the magnitude of systematic errors, across a number of data sources over a number of years, that would be necessary to alter the findings seems implausible.

The nine tables fall into two groups. Tables C–1 through C–5 report financial data (i.e., dollars of expenditure or asset value); Tables C–6 through C–9 show amounts of real resources associated with the various dollar values, and the amount of student "demand" for those resources. Moreover, certain of the tables (Tables C–2, C–3, C–5, and C–7) are secondary tables that translate per-pupil data into percentage distributions across the six institutional groups. The primary tables focus on the amount of resources available to students at a given type of institution; the secondary tables focus on how successfully the various groups are competing both for students and for resources.

Operating Expenditures

Looking first at the outcomes of UNC's "current" operations (Tables C–1 through C–3), two patterns emerge as particularly important. First, while real per-pupil operating expenditures increased for the system as a whole from 1964–66 to 1970–72, they remained constant from 1970–72 to 1976–78 (i.e., actual increases in total dollars spent were offset by inflation and enrollment increases). This pattern of constant per-pupil funding during the second time period did not hold true for every campus, however: real per-pupil expenditures at TBIs declined slightly from 1970–72 to 1976–78, while those at comparable TWIs increased. Moreover, real per-pupil expenditures for academic purposes declined dramatically at the TBIs, both in absolute and relative terms. Further, during both periods the share of total current funds allocated to general baccalaureate institutions and comprehensive institutions increased.

To see what all of this means, consider the changes in the combined operating expenditures of the three TBI general baccalaureate campuses compared to those of the three TWI general baccalaureate campuses. Between 1970–72 and 1976–78, the combined annual expenditures at the three TBIs increased from $7.2 million to $15.3 million. Of this increase, $4.6 million simply enabled these campuses to keep pace with higher salaries and higher prices. Of the remaining $3.5 million, only one-third ($1.3 million) went to additional academic resources. During this same period, full-time equivalent enrollment at these institutions increased from 3,650 to 5,470. This meant that the amount of resources per pupil was actually 13 percent less in 1978.

Total expenditures at the three TWIs increased by a slightly greater amount, from $7.4 million to $15.8 million, with $4.8 million being accounted for by inflation. In contrast to the TBIs, however, nearly two-thirds ($2.3 million) of the real increase went to additional academic resources at these campuses. Consequently, even though the three TWIs experienced slightly greater enrollment growth than the TBIs, they had 5 percent more academic resources per pupil in 1978 than they had had earlier.

The combined effect of these two changes is that although total net operating expenditures per pupil are now roughly equal, there are significant differences among institutional groups in the composition of those expenditures. In particular, the TBIs have significantly lower per-pupil expenditures for academic purposes than do comparable TWIs. Moreover, the fact that both these changes and current differences are real (i.e., not simply accounting differences) is supported by comparative data on student-faculty ratios and library book acquisitions. To continue our earlier illustration, for example, total full-time equivalent faculty at the three TBIs increased between 1970–72 and 1976–78 from 261 to 325, while faculty at the three TWIs increased during the same period from 267 to 381—about twice the TBI increase.

Capital Stock and Expenditures

A similar set of patterns emerges from examination of data on capital stock (i.e., physical plant and capital equipment) and capital expenditures (Tables C–4 and C–5). First, the value of capital stock per pupil increased overall between 1962–64 and 1970–72. Between 1970–72 and 1976–78, however, increases in the total value of physical plant were more than offset by enrollment increases and inflation so that real value per pupil declined, both overall and for each institutional group except the general baccalaureate TWIs. The share of UNC's total property value accounted for by general baccalaureate institutions and by comprehensive institutions increased during both periods.

These tables also show that the TBIs lost considerable ground between 1970–72 and 1976–78. Their share of UNC's total assets declined slightly while the shares of the comparable TWIs increased 20 to 30 percent. In real terms this meant that the amount of capital assets per pupil at the TBIs declined by 15 to 30 percent while the assets per pupil at the comparable TWIs declined by no more than 10 percent and in some cases actually increased. These shifts occurred despite what appears to be a more equitable distribution of capital appropriations. However, these total appropriations data mask the fact that most of the funds appropriated to the TBIs went to repairing or renovating existing structures.

Looking at the end result in per-pupil terms, one might conclude that these differences simply reflect an effort to have the TWIs "catch up" to the TBIs, since in 1978 the various institutional groups appear to have roughly comparable amounts of physical plant per pupil. However, these data mask both differences in the composition of available space (by use and condition) at the different institutions and differences in the per-pupil demand placed on "academic" space at the different institutions. Using the most educationally oriented measure ("net assignable square feet of instructional space in satisfactory condition per student credit hour"), TBIs are significantly worse off than comparable TWIs. Put in less abstract terms, the TBIs may have comparable dormitories and large administration buildings, but students at these campuses will sit in much more crowded and run-down classrooms.[5]

The Budgetary Process

As noted above, UNC's resource allocation decisions are, in some way, all linked to the process of developing a budget for the University. This process, which is typical of that for most state universities, is a joint venture of the State's Budget Office, the Legislature, the UNC Board of Governors, its general administration, and administrators at the sixteen campuses. Since the consolidation of UNC and the creation of a Board of Governors, the budget has been treated legislatively as a single entity (officially, it is the budget for the Board of Governors), although all of the funds in the budget are earmarked for specific institutions. Actually there are three distinct budgets: one for continuing operations (i.e., for providing funding of existing programs and services to existing numbers of students), another for funding new programs or additional students, and a third to fund capital projects.

Although the process is highly structured, and the roles of participants are well defined, it is clear that there is a considerable amount of informal cooperative effort, with the Board of Governors, the general administration, and the executive and legislative branches of state government working closely together. The State Legislature has the final say on the "bottom line" and, to some extent, on how funds are allocated within each of the three budgets. However, the Board of Governors has the final say in reconciling differences between the original request and the legislated budget. In making these final allocations, the Board relies heavily on information supplied to it by the general administration. These allocations, like the approved budget, are expressed in real, as well as dollar, terms. They include, for example, authorizations for specific numbers of faculty and other staff of various types, for the number of students to be served, and for the undertaking of specific capital projects.

Three characteristics of this budgetary process contributed substantially to the disparities identified above. First, separate funding for "continuing operations" and "enrollment expansion or new programs" provides that no campus will ever lose what it already has (on a per-pupil basis), so that any relative changes in budgets among the campuses must result from some campuses growing faster in enrollment or receiving relatively more "new program" money. Second, increases in authorized enrollment levels and proposals for new programs both require approval by the Board of Governors, whose criteria for judging such changes tended to favor already expanding campuses. And third, funds for additional administrative or student services were treated as comparable to funds for new academic programs, because the only dollar measure used to assess the equity of allocations was total per-pupil spending.

As described in earlier chapters, UNC created a set of readily expandable campuses from 1963 to 1972. And its budget mechanisms in subsequent years served only to add to the attractiveness of these campuses. With modern physical plants, well designed and staffed administrative organizations, and little debt service, these campuses could use their share of new monies for expanding existing academic programs, or adding new ones.

At the same time, much of the TBIs' share of these funds (which was smaller to begin with) went to providing needed additional student support services and to upgrading the administrations of these campuses to make them comparable to the TWIs. Given the constraint that additional funds per pupil at the TBIs be no higher than at the TWIs,[6] funding of academic activities clearly had to suffer. Though UNC officials deny any conscious trade-off between academic and non-academic spending, the outcome noted earlier is clear: spending for academic purposes declined at the TBIs, both in terms of amount per pupil and as a percentage of total spending at these campuses. Referring again to our comparison of TBI and TWI general baccalaureate campuses, total funding at both groups of campuses more than doubled between 1970–72 and 1976–78 (an increase of 50 percent in real terms), but funding for academic purposes increased at an even faster rate (up 120 percent) at the TWIs. Thus by 1978, these three institutions were spending 60 cents out of every dollar on academic resources (compared to 57 cents in 1970–72). In contrast, academic funding grew much more slowly at the TBIs (up 85 percent), so that in 1978 they were spending only 53 cents of each dollar on academic resources (compared with 60 cents in 1970–72).

CONNECTIONS WITH DESEGREGATION

The bottom line of the above comparison is clear: the TWIs have more educational resources to make available to students than do their TBI counterparts; moreover, this pattern is one which has not improved over the last several years. One consequence of these disparities is equally clear: they have had the effect of perpetuating racial duality. Whether intended or not, the TBIs have become less competitive as educational institutions and hence are less able to attract quality students. Indeed, some TBIs are having trouble attracting any students at all. Moreover, this disadvantage not only has persisted despite UNC's announced goals to the contrary, but also it becomes self-reinforcing under the North Carolina funding process where new dollars for program development go largely where the students are. That is, the relatively greater ability of the TWIs to attract students now becomes a rationale for authorizing new programs at these campuses, rather than at TBIs; in turn, these new programs attract more students, and the disparity is perpetuated.

In addition, this situation is made worse by recent (and projected future) declines in the college applicant pool, increasingly forcing UNC's constituent institutions to compete against one another for the same student. As a result, unless current practices are changed substantially, the status of the TBIs can be expected to worsen continually, a situation which is in itself a violation of Title VI (i.e., to simply close most, or all, of the TBIs is not viewed by the court as a legitimate way to end racial duality, so that the relative well-being of the TBIs matters, along with the relative well-being of the individual black students).

A second consequence of the existing resource disparities is much less obvious, but probably also much more important for the government's litigation against UNC: to reverse this pattern of decline will require either substantial new funds for the TBIs or else some type of program consolidation or relocation. Proposals for open enrollment, or even substantial financial incentives for students to attend TBIs, will not work. That is, for a significant number of students to shift to the TBIs, these campuses will have to acquire some sort of drawing power that the TWIs can't match. Even if they were free, however, the TBIs do not have classroom space or programs to offer potential new students.

The likelihood that the legislature would appropriate even the funds necessary to make the TBIs comparable, much less especially attractive, is significantly dependent upon the fiscal capacity of North Carolina taxpayers. And the likelihood that the TBIs can attract new students (i.e., individuals not now enrolled) is significantly dependent upon current enrollment rates. As Table 4–1 shows, North Carolina's limited wealth and current high tax effort, as well as its above-average enrollment rate, make any strategy for overcoming racial duality through enrollment expansion and increased fiscal support highly unrealistic.

Table 4–1
Comparison of North Carolina's Wealth, Enrollments, and Support
of Higher Education with Those of Selected Other States

States	Index of Taxable Wealth Per Capita	Enrollments per 1000 Population	Average State Appropriation Per Pupil	State Appropriation Per $1,000 of Personal Income
North Carolina	82.0	30.5	$4,156	$16.00
Other (9) States cited in *Adams*	93.6	26.3	3,694	11.20
Other (10) States in Southeastern U.S.	85.7	26.4	3,400	12.58
U.S. Average	100.0	29.0	3,682	10.64

Source: *Chronicle of Higher Education*, October 29, 1981 and February 10, 1982

THE UNC RESPONSE

The government's case against UNC was built around two provisions of the Title VI regulations:[7]

> [Institutions] may not . . . utilize criteria or methods of administration which have the effect of subjecting individuals to discrimination because of their race.

and

> The [institution] must take affirmative action to overcome the effects of prior discrimination.

The case involved an absolute and relatively straightforward interpretation of these regulations. The major thrust of its argument was that given a prior *de jure* segregated system, the simple demonstration of the continued existence of differentials in resource and enrollment (outcome) patterns across campuses constituted proof of Title VI violation.

The primary focus of UNC's defense against the government's charges was to challenge the validity of the government's interpretation of Title VI. This challenge centered around two themes: 1) identifying factors which, in UNC's view, limited its liability; and 2) showing why, again according to UNC, most of the "inequities" were of no *educational* consequence. On both topics, the arguments advanced by UNC addressed not only what criteria were most appropriate for judging its compliance with Title VI, but also what empirical evidence was most relevant.

In this section we will reexamine our earlier analysis in light of UNC's challenge to it. Our primary purpose in doing so is to show that that analysis stands up well to all of the defense's various challenges, even if the criteria for judging UNC's performance are extended to include consideration of factors such as student choice and educational efficiency. At the same time, it should also become clear that UNC's defense is not an attempt to dispute the government's evidence regarding the allocation of resources at UNC, but rather an effort to legitimize those allocations; as such, it provides a fairly comprehensive picture of the mechanisms which might be used to perpetuate racial segregation in higher education.

Limited Liability for Observed Outcomes

Part of UNC's challenge to the Title VI regulations was aimed at the "effect" clause:

> Does any resource allocation outcome constitute an "effect" of administration policies, or do only those outcomes which can be linked to the *intent*, or purpose, of those policies?

UNC sought to argue for the latter view. For example, one major defense witness asserted that declining TBI enrollments were not a function of their attractiveness (relative to TWIs), but were due to a combination of demographics and the fact that better-qualified blacks wanted to compete with the better-qualified students at TWIs.

The government, on the other hand, clearly presumed the broader definition to be the appropriate one. In response to the above assertion, for example, the government argued that UNC has a responsibility to do all it can to compensate for these factors.[8] In addition, the government asserted that it might also use available evidence on actual outcomes to argue that the "real" intent of UNC policies is different from the "stated" intent. The validity of this line of argument depends, at least in part, on whether UNC's administration can be expected to have estimates about what outcomes are likely—that is, even with some uncertainty and limited control, can they be held liable to utilize available statistical techniques? For example, should the administration be expected to know how students will respond to a given policy change? It certainly spends a lot of time modeling student enrollment. Even more, does the fact that, say, enrollment can only be forecast to plus or minus twenty-five students at any campus mean that "student enrollment choices are unknown" and can't be counted on?

It might be added here that UNC actually tried to have it both ways. On the one hand its witnesses argued that the lower college-going rate for blacks (compared with whites) could be attributed entirely to socioeconomic factors beyond UNC's control. At the same time, however, they also asserted that the higher college-going rate for blacks in North Carolina (compared with blacks in other *Adams* states) was entirely due to the outreach efforts of UNC.

The heart of UNC's challenge is a broad effort to establish limits on its legal liability for any observed outcomes. Its suggestions for limitations relate to a wide range of issues, possibly in the hope that if even one is accepted (and thus the principle established), drawing the line on further claims will be difficult.

For example, in what way does the prior existence of racial segregation affect UNC's liability? Should UNC have to take into account (i.e., compensate for) factors that it cannot fully control, such as white students' preferences for attending TWIs, but which are the product of prior discrimination? UNC's claims also extend to the separability of the violation and remedy aspects of litigation such as this. That is, does a finding of violation first require identifying a viable remedy? And, can the behavior of officials at the constituent institutions in UNC's allegedly "decentralized" decision process be viewed as another "external factor" limiting the central administration's control over resource allocation outcomes?

The key to understanding the disagreement here, as well as the disagreement (to be discussed later) concerning the mission of UNC as an educational institution, is to recognize the fundamental difference in approach between the University and the government. UNC's approach was that of a manager, focusing on the individual choices made by the UNC Board and the expressed purpose or rationale for those choices. The government's approach was that of an evaluator, focusing on the bottom line or net *effect* (i.e., outcome) of those choices. What is empirically significant about this difference is the fact that the equity implications of these actual outcomes were consistently different from the implications of the Board's stated intentions. Invariably, for example, actual levels of staffing and library books at the TBIs were less than their budgeted (authorized) levels.

This disagreement was about more than which stage in the UNC policy process should be the focus of this litigation. The view and approach of a manager—which UNC adopted—is a limited one. In particular, following the corporate tradition of American industry, the *liability* of managers is limited to only the most immediate, most direct effects of choices. Past mistakes are "sunk" costs; since they can't be undone, they are regarded as irrelevant to any new decisions. Moreover, these decisions typically are evaluated in terms of their effect on the "marginal" individual rather than in terms of some aggregate, or overall, effect. That is, for example, in analyzing the willingness of students to switch campuses following a program consolidation, managers consider the choice facing a student given the present student bodies (implying that only one student, or a few students would move), rather than considering what the two post-consolidation student bodies might look like. In addition, the math of the manager is accounting, with its philosophy that numbers are either all correct or they are wrong (and invalid).

The view of the evaluator, on the other hand, is one that focuses on the whole system, extending the liability of decisionmakers to include indirect or secondary effects that can be reasonably anticipated. In addition, the evaluator utilizes probability and statistics as the primary tool for processing data. These are tools that presume some inaccuracies in the data and explicitly address them. The appropriateness of these tools is closely tied to the evaluator's focus on the aggregate effect of policy choices rather than the consequences for a given individual. Much of UNC's criticism of the government's empirical evidence is directly tied to its managerial approach; for OCR, with a different perspective, these criticisms are largely meaningless.

Issues of Measurement and Methodology

The data-related discussion actually involved two components: issues of measurement and issues of methodology. The choice of measures was the dominant concern in the University's cross-examination of the government's key witness for the economic analyses.

With regard to the measures used, the examination focused on two recurring themes: the use of actual (as opposed to budgeted) expenditure data,[9] and the emphasis on patterns over time. The tables presented in Appendix C show how widely different measures of essentially the same phenomenon can vary. Similar differences exist between the government's and UNC's data on expenditures. In his questioning on this topic, the UNC defense attorney sought to create the impression that the government's numbers were "created" by its witness (and thus basically subjective rather than empirical values), and that since these were not (and, in some instances could not be) the measures used by the UNC administration in its decisionmaking, they could not meaningfully be used to describe those decisions.

This line of attack failed to recognize the *purpose* of the government's testimony. It was not to attempt to provide input to UNC's decisions, but rather to evaluate the consequences of those decisions. For example, the government's argument is not that "UNC chose to allocate to the 'TBI general baccalaureate schools' . . . ." but rather, "the *effect* of UNC's decisions on the TBI general baccalaureate institutions has been to . . ." And as for the "subjective" nature of the government's data, the defense's line of reasoning also failed to recognize that there is a substantial body of professional literature which supports the government's approach.[10] One essential feature of the approach is that it provides an independent check on UNC's policies. If only the data actually used by the administration were evaluated, this independence would be lost.

In contrast, the government's cross-examination of UNC witnesses shows that there is no inherent foundation for their choice of variables. In fact, their choices are shown to be largely *ad hoc*, self-serving, and not representative of any consistent underlying principles. For example, in offering evidence to support the argument that capital resources are being equitably distributed between the TBIs and the TWIs, UNC uses as a measure "total capital appropriation per new FTE student,"[11] implying that all capital expenditures go for new facilities to serve additional students at a given campus and that it does not matter whether the expenditure is for an academic facility or some ancillary service. Under such a measure the TBIs appear to get more than their share. However, this outcome actually reflects the fact that there was relatively little enrollment growth at the TBIs between 1972 and 1978, and it ignores the facts that nearly half of the TBIs' capital appropriations went to renovate existing facilities and that most of the new construction on these campuses was for administrative office space or dormitories. Both patterns are significantly different than those occuring at the TWIs.[12]

As OCR made clear, UNC also had no consistent framework for presenting time series data—the ten tables offered by UNC witnesses which included time series data covered eight different time periods; each starting date was the one that was most favorable to UNC's case. For example, in analyzing growth in appropriations for operating expenses, UNC uses the period 1968–1981—even though it argued previously that pre-1972 data should be ignored. In contrast, for capital appropriations, UNC asks the court to consider only 1973–1979, omitting years both at the beginning and the end which were much more favorable to the TWIs. A 1972–1981 time frame would have dramatically altered both sets of findings. The only justification offered was that "these were the data we had available," an assertion that was not always true.

Although this evidence added little directly to UNC's case, it probably did make a small indirect contribution. By showing that time series outcomes could be sensitive to the choice of a time period, and by following a highly subjective approach itself, UNC's testimony may have helped to reduce the weight attached by the court to any time series data. Together with the argument about the comparability of specific measures across campuses over time, it made clear the extreme vulnerability of time series analysis to this line of attack. That is, all of the flaws identified in UNC's evidence in effect become *potential* problems for the government's evidence; and establishing the existence simply of such potential is often adequate to create doubt.

The defense against such an attack requires both a clear a priori rationale for the choice of data points and a set of measures which can separate isolated occurrences or aberrations from basic underlying patterns. The government's evidence, in contrast to UNC's, in fact, did meet both of these requirements. As a result, the possibility of error and the potential magnitude of any error were reduced to relatively small numbers, but were not eliminated.

Though most of UNC's challenges to the government's data were on measurement issues, its criticism also extended to methodological issues. Particular attention was given to the way in which the raw data were aggregated to produce multi-year/multi-campus averages. As noted earlier, the same line of argument was followed as above: these averages are unusable by a manager as decisionmaking tools and thus provide no new information.

Student Choice

Much of the strength in UNC's claims that its liability should be limited depends on its ability to incorporate into the litigation both the findings and the perspective of the so-called "student choice" models that are currently receiving considerable play in the professional literature.

This student choice argument contains a number of distinct elements—all related to the significance of the fact that, unlike elementary and secondary students, college students are free to choose if and where they will attend college. Some of the elements focus on the factors that determine student behavior. In general, the greatest weight was attached to the effect college will have on a student's labor market status. In general, witnesses argued that institutional quality makes no difference—that graduates of the TBIs do as well, and are as satisfied as, comparable graduates of the TWIs.[13]

Another set of studies focused on the factors that determine the likelihood of a student's applying, enrolling, or graduating from a particular institution. These studies argue that student self-selection is at work—and that admissions policies are not an important constraint. Students choose schools where most students will have abilities and backgrounds similar to their own, and students are much less likely to graduate if their abilities are significantly below the average.[14] As to whether students know how well they will probably do, a number of witnesses assert that SAT scores and class rank are good predictors. All of these studies attached little significance to the educational services provided by an institution as a factor determining a student's enrollment choice, a student's performance, or a student's subsequent success in the labor market.[15]

The bottom line of this student choice argument, like that of the arguments related to UNC's administrative structure, is that UNC's liability for most resource outcomes is severely limited, and that these limitations must be taken into account in determining whether UNC is in violation of Title VI. In the University's view, it is not a violation to "accommodate" student preferences concerning whom they would like as fellow students, particularly if such accommodation does not reduce the total number of black graduates.

The arguments for rejecting this evidence as irrelevant are linked to the weaknesses of student choice models, which are conceptual as well as empirical. The most damaging point, given the government's view that the litigation should be focused on aggregate effects, is that these are micro models whose results are valid for an individual student, or a small group of students; they tell us little or nothing about large-scale changes. For example, they do not tell us whether significant increases in enrollment of blacks at TWIs, or in the numbers of blacks with college degrees in the labor market, would negate the studies' findings.[16] In addition, the absence of an accompanying framework to establish even observed micro-outcomes as general equilibrium makes it virtually impossible to know whether these observations reflect optimal choices or simply available supply. For example, do students not bother applying to schools where there's a good chance they will be rejected?[17]

Paralleling these conceptual problems are two key empirical weaknesses. One results from the fact that studies, such as those of David Wise, were not designed specifically to address the issues in this case (e.g., program consolidation to eliminate racial duality). Thus, for example, Wise uses a model, based on a sample of data for one point in time, to predict the consequences of a future change in a variable (program offerings) not even in his model in a situation where the racial identifiability of the institutions (also not in the model) may be important.[18] The other empirical weakness of these models is their reduced reliability as they are applied at a more disaggregated level than in their original studies. A study that shows a pattern of behavior representative of students of all ability levels attending all different types of institutions scattered throughout the nation is likely to tell us nothing about how students from one end of the ability spectrum attending a particular institution will respond to some given change.[19] The point that should be emphasized here is that one really has to stretch to make these models relevant— probably much farther than they can legitimately be stretched.[20]

In some cases, these problems were further compounded by bad scholarship. For example, a study by Arthur Padilla on the class of 1974 purports to show that graduates of the TWIs and TBIs were equally satisfied with their education. However, the attrition in his sample and the self-selection bias of respondents made such a finding virtually tautological. Similarly, Mickey Birnum's study, which allegedly shows that graduates of TBIs do as well as graduates of TWIs, is based on a sample of ten graduates of TBIs in 1962 who could still be located eleven years later—using a methodology designed for a nationally representative sample of 50,000 students to analyze less than 3,000 of those who responded to an eleven-year follow-up survey.[21]

The Role of the University

The effort to establish a very small domain of liability for the UNC administration went beyond these various empirically based arguments. Indeed, as an extension of its managers' approach to the issues directly linked to the litigation, the defense went on to challenge the view implicit in the government's case concerning the role of the University as an educational institution—that is, to argue that Title VI is not sound educationally.

This challenge, as it related to resource allocations, centered around two basic issues. The first of these involved the nature of the administration's authority and its basic objectives in managing the University. UNC officials sought to picture the role of the general administration as basically a *passive* one. They argued that the University's budgeting process (including both the funding of ongoing operations and the provision of funds for new programs, students, or capital) is essentially decentralized, with the primary initiative coming from each campus. The general administration and Board of Governors simply act as reviewers. Their role within this framework is to assess the requests of the constitutent institutions as they affect UNC as a whole. Moreover, it was asserted that this assessment was not based on the preferences of the general administration, but rather on the "needs" of pupils (as identified by the individual campuses) and what limited resources "were available" to UNC.

To assess the significance of these arguments, one must also take into account UNC's view of what it means to "meet students' needs." That view has two basic components. First, students' needs are seen to arise from the existing labor market status of potential students and the additional benefits they would obtain by attending UNC. In turn, UNC's primary objective here is to provide these potential students *access* to its resources.

A number of UNC's witnesses (especially its experts) argued that what is of primary importance for most black students is whether or not they had a college degree. The quality of the training represented in those degrees was said to be inconsequential. The University's position on this issue is perhaps best summarized by the following excerpt from the cross-examination of its highest-priced expert:

Q. You believe, do you not, that, in fact, there is no black college or university in this country that ranks with a decent state university, do you not?

A. Yes.

Q. And do you believe that black colleges fail academically prepared students who do, in fact, attend black colleges in substantial numbers?

A. Yes.

Q. In fact, you believe they do a miserable job of developing the potential of academically prepared students, do you not?

A. Yes.

As for the second component, access was seen to be directly related to applications, enrollments, and persistence in college. Any action that reduced these factors for black students would be discriminatory, and actions that improved them would constitute evidence of racially fair behavior. In this regard, various UNC administrators all presented examples of how much UNC does, in fact, to recruit, enroll, and retain black students.[22] And UNC's experts all testified that their respective studies suggest that efforts to consolidate programs would reduce the number of black students who earn UNC degrees.[23]

Two logical extensions of this line of reasoning presented by UNC are that, in looking at what actually happens, it is more useful to look at program effects than program inputs; and that programs are defined as much by the students enrolled in them as by the resources provided for them by UNC. Again, the UNC imputation is clear: OCR's focus on resource allocations per se is misplaced. In the view of UNC, additional resources are allocated where there is an "identified need": that is, students who could benefit from the additional resources in the sense of performing better after graduation. Since highly qualified students are more likely to realize such benefits, it is appropriate to allocate them additional resources. Only after "correcting" for such differences in "need" is it meaningful to compare staffing levels across campuses.

UNC's view of itself as administratively decentralized also extends to actual program operations (i.e., to the utilization of budgeted resources). The central administration's role in these operations is seen as one of coordinating program management and planning. Its management control extends only to *authorizing* (i.e., making available) resources for use by the various campuses, and its planning must be based on authorized (i.e., "budgeted") enrollment levels. A corollary argument is that to determine the quantity of resources *available*, one should look at revenues rather than expenditures and that the best measure of *total resources* available is the sum of tuition receipts plus state appropriations.

Though a seemingly minor point, this argument has a number of important implications. For one, it supports the view that the general administration has a largely *passive* role in UNC's resource allocation; its appropriation for any campus is simply a residual, the amount of need not covered by tuition receipts. In turn, what little control it has is seen to come from only authorizing expenditures that are educationally sound (efficient). Furthermore, it is argued that to properly perform this duty, the administration is "forced" to give priority to present conditions over any possible past inequities.

Simply to give additional resources to the TBIs, which have not sought to argue the need for such resources, would be wasteful (and thus harmful), said UNC. Financial Vice President Felix Joyner argued that any unilateral initiative by the general administration would be wasteful. This view, of course, ignores the fact that years of discrimination may have taught the TBIs to expect very little.

Educational Soundness of Title VI

The logical consequences of this line of reasoning for the TBIs are clear: relative enhancement would be wrong. Indeed, one direct implication of this line of reasoning is that *the less attractive the TBIs become for good students, the better off poor blacks will be.* This argument has a strong economic flavor. It implies that the benefits of a college degree are reflected predominantly, if not solely, in later increased earnings. In turn, it implies that these benefits are not the product of any acquired cognitive skills, but rather are the result either of students' learning good habits (disciplined behavior that can be transferred to the workplace) or simply passing through a labor market "screen."

To effectively challenge the validity of these labor market out-

comes is likely to be impossible, for existing data typically are consistent with several hypotheses.[24] However, the most appropriate
challenge is to the relevance of this entire line of argument. UNC's
mission is to provide educational services, not simply higher wages
after graduation. Thus, of greater importance than UNC's claim that
it is "doing all it can to recruit, enroll and graduate" blacks is whether
it is doing all it can *educationally* for black students—for example, in
ensuring comparable programs, or appropriate remedial and other
support services, or an integrated environment (as measured in terms
of resources, services, courses, staff, and so forth). In the context of
program consolidation proposals, this last question becomes, "Are
there specific remedial or support services that must accompany such
consolidations to enable students with differing academic backgrounds and abilities to benefit jointly from a given program?"

The second focus of UNC's educational arguments involved the
relative priority that should be given to "efficiency" in the allocation
of educational resources. The managers' view is that efficiency considerations must take priority, in effect operating as a constraint on
efforts to increase equity. Implicitly, such a position takes the existing
allocation as the legitimate starting point (i.e., sunk costs are sunk
costs) in asserting that short-run educational costs for some students
cannot be justified by possible long-run benefits to others. (This, of
course, would include any remedy that creates temporary disloca-
tions by consolidating programs). Here, "efficiency" takes on a second dimension: the avoidance of new costs (e.g., dislocation costs
associated with program consolidation). As a result, "efficiency"
comes more to mean, in part, "preservation of the status quo." Moreover, UNC suggested that evidence on the racial composition of
enrollments should not be given the same weight as it is in elementary
and secondary litigation (where pupils are assigned to schools); and
"remedies" should not be evaluated solely, or even primarily, on
racial mix grounds.

In addition, UNC argued that its performance should be judged
in relation to the other *Adams* states, in part to account for various
intangible factors that effectively limit just how much change a university can accomplish in a given period of time. This argument is
reinforced by UNC's general argument that the current period is the
only relevant one.

The broader perspective of the evaluator would reject the current
allocation as the only legitimate starting point and would focus on
the long-run rather than short-run efficiency consequences. That is,
short-run costs that accrue to those who have benefited from past
discrimination might be discounted, or even ignored—students required to transfer from TWIs to TBIs because of program consoli-

dation or relocation would fall into this category. Such a transfer would be "inefficient" only if over the long run it implied the need for more resources to provide the same services.[25] Such an outcome is very unlikely if it is also the case that these services are being provided to similar students.

However, UNC argued that, in addition to short-run dislocation costs, the greater diversity of students would produce just such extra costs, as well as reduced educational benefits for black students. The basis for these arguments is, again, the student choice literature. The loss-of-benefit argument is explicit in this literature: because they would have to compete with better-qualified students, more blacks would fail to graduate, resulting in a "waste" of UNC's limited resources.

Again, this argument is based on the premise that UNC's "output" is not educational services but labor market outcomes, and that such outcomes are unrelated to the services provided by UNC. The extra-cost argument, on the other hand, is generally only implied: students of widely differing abilities would require significantly different educational inputs or approaches to achieve a given output. None of the articles cited in UNC's testimony, however, offer any explicit analysis of the relationship between inputs and outputs. Moreover, the testimony completely ignored the fact that the changes implied in the remedies proposed by the government (not to mention the context within which the changes are being proposed) are simply not covered by the findings of these studies.

Similarly, UNC's argument also ignored the possibility that the educational "compatibility" of students can be altered. Drawing on the literature of Coleman and others, this issue might be put as, "Is there some 'optimal' heterogeneity in the classroom?" And, "Is this 'optimal' spread a function of the given program, or the instructor, or the availability of support services?" Alternatively, the policy question might be framed as, "What can UNC do to maximize, or at least increase, this 'spread'?" Clearly there may be extra costs associated with program consolidation or relocation, but these would be more than offset by cost savings resulting from the elimination of degree program duplication and through increased benefits accruing to black students.

IMPLICATIONS AND CONCLUSIONS

Although the resource allocation dimension of this litigation does involve "harder" data than most other dimensions of the case, it is no less subjective. It is clear from the above discussion that differences in basic assumptions both with regard to civil rights and to education are at the heart of the disagreements. Moreover, while there are at least three distinct issues, their significance is largely a function of how they relate to one another.

Thus, the threefold defense of UNC is actually one argument with several faces—at least in part, this approach seems based on the belief that a sufficiently distracting defense can help to create doubt about the prosecution's case. Moreover, the very interrelationships among issues become part of the defense: the arguments for efficiency depend heavily on the "promoting access" objective, and in turn, are key contributions to UNC's claim of "limited liability for outcomes." Moreover, "access" is equated with "opportunity." In this context, the goal of "equalizing educational *opportunity*" is then alleged to have three implications:

1. UNC must not base policies solely on their consequences for a particular subpopulation, but must take into account the potential impact on all students.

2. UNC policies must not "constrain" any group of students (taking existing conditions as a reference point); and

3. UNC policies must not "waste" educational resources, thereby reducing the total amount of "opportunity" it can make available.

Moreover, since these implications influence the outcome of UNC's policies in a relatively complicated way, UNC argued that the focus for evaluating its performance should be on what it is trying to do, rather than what it actually accomplishes[26]—and, following a similar logic, that "trying" is best reflected in its stated plans and procedures, rather than the actual implementation of those plans and procedures.

In sum, UNC argued that to show violation of Title VI, the government must simultaneously show: 1) planned resource disparities (which are significant beyond doubt) among the constituent institutions; and 2) alternative allocations that could have been made within the University's operating framework and that would have represented both more access to the University's resources by blacks and no less "efficiency" in the utilization of those resources. Given that UNC policies and decisions never mention race, it would be difficult to prove that any of its actions were for the purpose of discriminating. But, more important, the second argument precludes significant relative enhancement of the TBIs (because it would make them too competitive for some blacks) and also precludes taking away any existing programs or resources from TWIs (because a disruption would be inefficient). Almost by definition, then, UNC is "doing all it can."

Finally, the real significance of the various UNC arguments stems from their collective impact, particularly as they relate to UNC's historical liability, on where the burden for proving or disproving violation lies and on the relative importance to be given to the effects of UNC policy on black students as a whole and the traditionally black institutions themselves, as opposed to simply the "marginal" black student. The first two particulars (i.e., the existence of a prior *de jure* segregated system and whether outcome data alone are sufficient to establish liability) are essentially legal issues; the basic concern underlying both is whether the regulations written to implement Title VI and the Revised Criteria issued by the *Adams* court are consistent with the legislation itself. The third point, on the other hand, is more substantive and more focused on the educational dimension of this case.

The thrust of UNC's challenge here is that Title VI is unsound educational policy whose literal implementation would be harmful to all students, black as well as white. In turn, this challenge, as well as UNC's position on the first two points, is completely dependent on acceptance of its view concerning the nature and role of the University.

NOTES

1. This is same data base which underlies much of the two previous chapters. It should also be pointed out that disputes related to the data base itself comprised a major (time-wise), but completely separate, dimension of the case—this dimension is treated to some extent in the next section.

2. In fact, nearly one-fourth of the testimony related to these tables involved describing their construction. It should be added that defense efforts to discredit the resulting tables failed to produce any evidence to suggest that the figures contained in them were in any way fallacious or simply statistical artifacts. In short, the tables do say what they claim to say.

3. More recent data was subsequently made available. The significance of these new figures is examined both in the next section and in the next chapter.

4. The set of measures used here is not only the one most likely to be used by other economists; it is also the most common choice of financial analysts. Moreover, the averaging of multiple years of data and the use of real, rather than nominal, values are generally regarded as good economics.

5. This interpretation is clearly more consistent with the descriptions of various campuses presented in Chapter Two than is UNC's interpretation of comparability.

6.   The asymmetry in the specification of this constraint reflects the fact that it only seems to have been used to explain that only the TBIs could not be allocated larger sums in a given year.

7.   Federal Register, Vol. 45, No. 92 (May 9, 1980), p. 30918.

8.   A corollary of this issue is whether the importance of "unintended" effects also depends on their being "adverse" effects.

9.   In its direct testimony, this issue took the form of using revenues (tuition receipts plus appropriations) rather than expenditures; the analysis, in both cases, is the same.

10.   See Note 6.

11.   This measure appears both in the testimony offered by Felix Joyner and in the "Comparative Study."

12.   The most dramatic difference between the TBIs and the comparable TWIs, in terms of capital construction, is the number of new academic buildings constructed at the two groups of campuses during the 1970s. There were nearly three times as many projects at the TWIs as there were at the TBIs.

13.   Most studies of student behavior find the "whether-or-not-to-en-roll" decision closely linked to expected labor market payoffs. But in choosing among colleges, other factors are usually found to come into play. And a number of recent studies have shown program quality to be significant. These issues (and the studies by UNC) are discussed further in the next section.

14.   See David Wise, "New Evidence on the Economic Determinants of Post-Secondary Schooling Choices," with W.C. Fuller and C.F. Manski, working paper, April 1980; also Stephen P. Dresch and A. L. Weldenberg, "Labor Market Incentives, Intellectual Competence and College Attendance," IDES, March 1978; and articles in Lewis C. Solomon and Paul J. Taubman, *Does College Matter?* New York: Academic Press, 1973.

15.   This includes the methodologically sound studies, such as those done by David Wise, as well as those which are simply bad scholarship, such as the studies done by Arthur Padilla and Mickey Birnum.

16.   It is not unreasonable to argue that the payoff to black students with *any* degree reflects their relative scarcity in the labor market and the corresponding ability of employers to use such a requirement as a "screen." As a larger number of blacks receive degrees, this screen will no longer be useful.

17.   For poorer students, application fees are significant. It should also be noted that studies which show that many who did not apply would have been accepted tell us nothing about specific program preferences, or special circumstances of applicants, or of the risk-taking behavior of applicants.

18.   In addition to relying on cross-sectional data, Wise also uses two *reduced-form* models. The problem with a reduced-form model is that while it can estimate the net effect of simultaneous changes in a number of factors, it cannot reveal "why" that effect occurred, because the respective contri-

butions of the various factors cannot be isolated. In fact, if one allows for the possibility of measurement error, then the reduced-form model cannot even say whether or not one factor is more important than another. For example, while Wise's results show that SAT score is more important than family income in "explaining college attendance or persistence," this may simply be a function of SAT scores being measured more accurately than family incomes. Moreover, his use of a "micro-model" to address aggregate policy questions is a significant flaw, in part, because Wise appears to assume that the "supply" of spaces in the University is not fixed, but rather, the University establishes criteria and then accepts whoever meets those criteria. (A "queuing" model—where institutions accept the first so-many applicants in the queue—may be much more informative here; one test of this alternative specification would be determining whether student application and enrollment patterns change with formalized open enrollment.)

19. Again, Wise admits this weakness, although he appears to act as though it is not fatal. He also admits that none of the models (his own included) work well in explaining relationships at the extremes of the ability distribution (and many UNC students fall into these ranges).

20. Wise explicitly admits these studies are not applicable to a "single university." But he does not hesitate to then go on to draw policy conclusions about North Carolina.

21. See Mickey Birnum, "The Earnings Effect of Black Matriculation in Predominantly Black Colleges," *Industrial and Labor Relations Review* (July 1980); and Arthur D. Padilla, "the Class of 1974; Early Careers of Graduates from the Sixteen Campuses of the University of North Carolina," UNC, 1978. It should also be noted that both authors used a common argument to defend their methodological weaknesses: "This was a *path-breaking* study."

22. See Chapter Two.

23. See, for example, David A. Wise, "The Effects of SAT Scores, High School Performance and Labor Market Opportunities on College Application, Quality and Admissions," with S. Venti, Working Paper, March 1980. He extends the analysis in this paper to argue that any consolidation of programs would be bad for less able blacks because even though they may be provided better educational resources, having to compete with more able students will mean that fewer will graduate.

24. It might be pointed out here, however, that there is a body of literature related to institutional measures of college quality which UNC witnesses ignore, and which has very different implications for UNC's case.

25. Short-run dislocation costs, in effect, are seen not as educational costs (i.e., costs of providing educational services) but as costs of overcoming the racial identifiability of the constituent institutions.

26. UNC utilizes such "names" as Robin Fleming, Donald Smith, and David Henry to legitimize this view.

CHAPTER **5**

The Consequences of the Consent Decree

We pointed out in Chapter One that Judge Pratt found the University of North Carolina in violation of the Civil Rights Act as long ago as 1973. That finding was affirmed several times over the next six years. Under Title VI of the Act, the University has an affirmative duty to remove all vestiges of a previously *dual* system, one white and one black, as a condition of receipt of federal funds. The duty to desegregate is affirmative in nature, and the mere adoption of racially neutral policies for student applicants is not adequate to remedy the consequences of past discrimination. As the court put it years earlier in *Morris v. State Council of Higher Education* (404 U.S. 908, 1971), a state's duty is to "convert its white colleges and black colleges into just colleges."

UNC never took this step and never made credible plans for taking it in the future. This much was established in the court record by 1979, when Charles Morgan and Joseph Levin took the matter of a final hearing over terminating $100 million a year in federal funds into the Raleigh courtroom of Judge F.T. Dupree, Jr. There, they claimed that compliance had been achieved and they asked Dupree to enjoin (that is, to prohibit) the hearing. In June 1979, Judge Dupree ruled that HEW must defer its plan to withhold federal aid until an administrative law hearing was held. He also denied UNC's motion to enjoin the hearing and he asserted continuing jurisdiction over the outcome.

The hearing began in July 1980 and continued into June 1981

before administrative law Judge John Mathias, with UNC styled technically as the respondent and LDF as intervenor. (LDF represented the plaintiffs in *Adams v. Richardson*, but they were not party to the suit brought by UNC before Judge Dupree—a part of Morgan's legal maneuvering. They were subsequently permitted by the administrative law judge who later disqualified himself to intervene in the hearing, over the objections of UNC.) In that year of proceedings, about 15,000 pages of testimony and over 500 exhibits were placed into the record.

The schedule established by Judge Mathias called for final rebuttal by OCR to begin in July 1981 and to extend for a month or two at most. The affirmative cases for both OCR and UNC had been completed. Mathias planned to study the record and issue an opinion some time between October and December 1981.

Very soon after the inauguration of Ronald Reagan in January 1981, and nearly *as if* by agreement reached during the presidential election campaign (given the highly proactive involvement of Senator Jesse Helms in the politics of the dispute), Education Secretary Terrel H. Bell named a private attorney who had served as a counselor in the Ford White House, Douglas F. Bennett, to advise him and to serve as counselor in negotiating a draft consent decree between OCR and UNC.

The quest for a consent decree is commonplace in civil suits and administrative law proceedings of all kinds. Indeed, HEW and OCR and UNC together had tried to reach a consent agreement on two occasions before March 1979, and had failed. What was unusual this time was that the effort was kept secret, even from all of the OCR attorneys except Richard Foster, and that the negotiations were conducted between Bennett and in-house legal counsel for UNC President William Friday, with Richard Foster and a few others participating, while the other attorneys from Morgan and Associates, OCR, and LDF continued their work on the hearing.

Secretary Bell announced the achievement of a draft consent decree on June 20, 1981, stating in a press release that did not include the draft that "the progress in this case exemplifies what can be accomplished by good faith negotiations," and reminding the media that "since assuming office as Secretary of Education, I have used every available opportunity to express publicly my deep commitment to reducing the extent of federal intrusion in state affairs . . . I am confident we will be able to point to other successes in the future. . . . The State will control the destiny of its own distinguished and respected University."

LDF objected to the draft decree in three courts: before Judge Dupree, before Judge Pratt of the District Court in Washington, D.C., and before the Washington, D.C. U.S. Court of Appeals. Although a few small changes were made in the draft decree in the course of its judicial review, LDF's objections were swept aside in the course of its overall acceptance by Judge Dupree. The Court of Appeals voted 2 to 1 to not review the case because it was from another circuit. A year later, the dissenting opinion written by Judge Skelly Wright and fashioned after the arguments of Joseph Rauh, induced the same Court to rehear the case *en banc* in 1983. The consent decree is thus at risk, and the twelve-year-old case of *Adams* lives on!

The work of the Abt Associates team, which had been slated to serve as the foundation for the rebuttal, was within two weeks of completion at the time of the draft decree's completion, and OCR quite naturally terminated further analysis and planning as of June 30, 1981. This final chapter is based on a fitting of the Abt team's rebuttal preparations to the contents of the decree, with a view to gauging whether implementation of the decree will result in desegregating the UNC campuses and in ending the remaining vestiges of discrimination. Using the knowledge gained from concerted study of the evidence and the issues, we will close this book in the way social scientists are trained to finish—by sharing with readers their forecasts of some of the traceable consequences that are likely to unfold during this decade *if and when* the decree is implemented.

Where history suports the forecasts, the authors expect that the credibility given to their initial lines of analysis will increase. Where it disconfirms them, future researchers and policymakers can gain by interpreting for themselves where the basic analysis went wrong or was faulty. The forecast has not presumed to control for "emergents"—unanticipated changes in political direction or in state practices that come up out of the seedbeds of local subcultures, including those of the university itself. We have presupposed a short-term future of the 1980s, much like the period of the 1970s spanned by the *Adams* decision.

The forecasts concern three main features of the decree: student recruitment, degree program changes, and equality of student access. These are viewed as the major operative policy factors in the decree. We are not concerned with such other considerations as the fact that, in the words of the decree,

> The University's compliance with this Decree shall be measured solely by a standard of good faith efforts to achieve and implement the goals and commitments of this Decree. . . . Non-performance of specific actions or nonattainment of specific numerical goals caused by external factors that are beyond the control of the plaintiffs (UNC), such as significantly altered eco-

nomic or demographic conditions, shall not result in a finding
of noncompliance . . .[1]

Nor are we concerned with Secretary Bell's more candid interpretation of this and related clauses, when he announced:

> These numerical goals are set with the clear understanding
> that failure to meet them is not automatically to be deemed failure
> to comply with the agreement. . . . Flexibility on the goals will
> ensure that they are not interpreted as rigid quotas at some time
> in the future.

Bell offered this interpretation not only to assure the American
public that performance would not be monitored closely or narrowly
but also to cope with the politically ticklish difficulty that the degree
establishes a few definite racial percentages and in doing so contra-
dicts the pledge of the Reagan Administration to eliminate quotas in
equity and affirmative action policies.

Finally, our effort at forecasting does not concern itself with the
fact that the decree was ordered by Judge Dupree to remain in effect
until December 31, 1988, reserving jurisdiction to himself for that
period in the event that any party began proceedngs to seek compliance or other relief. In other words, the decree was designed to
seal off revision or new litigation for a period of at least six and a
half years. This feature of the decree, in fact, simply reinforces con-
fidence in the operative portions of the decree as constituting both
the parts and the sum of what will be done within UNC during the
1980s. Finally, the decree is *now* in effect and will continue until the
Court of Appeals finishes its reconsideration, if not indefinitely.

MINORITY ENROLLMENT

The decree states that by 1987, the year before the decree ceases to
be in force, "minority presence enrollment shall equal or exceed
15.0% of the total combined headcount enrollment in the predominantly black institutions and shall equal or exceed 10.6% of the total
combined headcount enrollment in the predominantly white institutions." These are the only specific percentage guidelines mentioned. None is set for graduate and professional students except as
they meld into the overall enrollments and none is set for faculty or
administrative hiring and redistribution except as contained in a pledge
to prepare periodic affirmative action hiring goals.

The goal of 10.6 percent black students at the ten TWIs combined after the next five years can be accomplished with ease. Assuming no change in total enrollment, the number of black students at TWIs would have to grow from 6,769 in 1979 to 10,051 in 1987, for an increase of about 3,470. Three out of ten white campuses, including two of the very largest, already meet or exceed the goal. And, since headcount—not full-time registration—is the category, it will not matter whether the black newcomers enroll for one course a term or five.

The goal of 15 percent white students at the five TBIs by 1987 would mean a growth from 1,492 whites in 1979 to 2,453 in 1987, if total enrollments remain constant. This *cannot* be accomplished unless significant new incentives are introduced, particularly when it is slated to occur simultaneously with the TWI actions. We return to this forecast later in this chapter.

STUDENT RECRUITMENT

The decree expends many pages in listing the ways in which UNC will recruit blacks onto white campuses and whites onto black campuses. The contents were earlier presented in 1980 in lengthy testimony by Admissions Officers and Vice Chancellors for Student Affairs from TWI campuses.

The essence is that some UNC campuses, especially Chapel Hill, have already adopted practices of publicity, visitation, orientation materials, family stayovers on campus, financial aid, and flexible admissions standards, among other devices, in recruiting black undergraduates. These practices *work*, but are far from sufficient in themselves. They deserve to be installed on every campus in the system. They will stimulate movement toward the goal of 10.6 percent black students at TWIs, although that goal will be reached or exceeded on some campuses (Chapel Hill, State, East Carolina, Greensboro) and will not be even approximated at others by these means (Asheville, Appalachia, and Western).

Because other remedies are missing, however, student recruitment will place at a further disadvantage three of the five TBIs (A&T, Elizabeth City, and Winston-Salem). These TBI campuses will not have the resources to compete in outreach with many of the TWIs. Thus, their recruitment efforts will lag behind some TWIs, who will cut deeply into the old markets for TBI-bound blacks. *Three of the five TBIs will not become 15% white.*

The latest population projections available from UNC *reverse* earlier planning based on continuing annual growth in enrollments through 1990.[2] The decree asserts that enrollments will decline after

1986 and that the rate of decline will be greater for blacks than for whites. If there will be 16,976 fewer black twenty- to twenty-four-year olds in 1990 than in 1979, that will be 12 fewer recruitable black students per 100 for UNC. If TWIs are to recruit 4,000 more blacks by about 1990 than they do now, and if their market competitiveness relative to TBIs is as great as we think it is, then the impasse for several TBI campuses is obvious. The same latest population report forecasts 39,592 fewer whites by 1990, or a loss of 9 per 100 available in 1979. (In spite of these new projections, UNC has planned for a slight enrollment increase from 1981 to 1986.)

One other forecast can be made: federal funds for student aid will be reduced between 1982 and 1985. At UNC, those funds are critically essential to recruiting black students, twice as many of whom proportionally are in financial need. The new competition for black students will thus be doubly hampered, by population declines and by unmet financial needs. This strain will be compounded on enrollments in the upper-division grades of students who are part-time, working commuters.

The combination of an influx of older, more nontraditional students, reduced financial aid, and higher tuition leads us to predict that more UNC students will attend college part-time and that more will seek to live at home. This will make the campuses in metropolitan areas, where the local economies offer better job opportunities, more magnetic. In our judgment, among the fifteen campuses, several TWIs, particularly Charlotte, Greensboro, and Wilmington, will benefit from this trend.

The significance of a decline in financial aid for low-income students cannot be overstated. It could in itself prove disastrous for the future viability of the TBIs. As Table 5–1 shows, students at the TBIs rely on federal help much more heavily than do students at comparable TWIs. At the black baccalaureate campuses, for example,

Table 5–1
Importance of Federal Student Aid at Selected UNC Campuses, 1978–79

Institutional Group	Total Enrollment	Percent of Students Who Receive		Total Federal Student Aid as a Percent of	
		Any Student Aid	BEOG	Total Student Costs	All Student
General Baccalaureate					
TBIs	6,029	83.5	69.1	64.5	76.8
TWIs	8,127	73.0	19.2	14.6	36.1
Comprehensive					
TBIs	8,873	89.1	58.3	42.3	78.9
TWIs	13,053	47.1	16.3	11.8	35.9

nearly two-thirds of all student costs (including tuition, required fees, room and board, and books and supplies) are paid for with federal dollars. Moreover, these federal dollars will not easily be replaced, as they currently account for over three-quarters of all student aid at these campuses.

The potential impact of a reduction in federal assistance is further compounded by the recent increases in tuition at all UNC campuses. These increases, ranging from 12 to 20 percent, provided most of the funds for the increases approved in the UNC budget. In following this path, the General Assembly warned that it might do so again in order to fund any further budget growth. Under these conditions, the promises for student recruitment outreach in the decree will not work to desegregate the UNC system.

Degree Programs

The second "remedial" strategy adopted by the decree is that of adding degree programs to TBIs. According to the press conference news release, twenty-nine degree programs will be added between 1981 and 1983. These include the twenty-seven listed in the UNC *Long Range Plan, 1981–1985,* completed in December 1980. We have tabulated those twenty-nine programs in Table 5–2. These programs were *authorized* by the Board of Governors. That does not mean funds will be allocated for staffing or equipping the programs.

Most of the newly authorized degree programs, which achieved that status in 1980, not as a result of the decree bargaining, are steps taken toward program *parity.* That is to say, they are steps that help equalize study opportunities at TBIs relative to the TWIs. The engineering entries at A&T, for instance, merely authorize a rounding out of that school's basic offerings in a way that will make it a fairly complete school rather than a severely truncated one relative to the TWIs.

The flaw in the list rests in its weakness as a remedial tool. Only two of the twenty-nine degree programs have some magnetic prospect because they are not duplicated elsewhere on other UNC campuses. These are animal science at A&T and recreation therapy at Winston-Salem. (There are course offerings elsewhere, but not many.) If we assumed these were in place and functioning well, they might have an effect on a combined total of 100 white students a year.

Because of Fayetteville's location in a growing metro area and because of its own small successes in attracting some whites in 1979 and 1980, the six new degree programs there, if funded and implemented, could increase the desegregative and academic viability of

Table 5-2
Newly Authorized Degree Programs

Degree Program		TBI					TWI							
Type	Specific	A&T	NCCU	FSU	WSSU	ECSU	UNC-C	UNC-G	WCU	UNC-A	UNC-CH	ECU	UNC-W	NCSA
Management	Accounting	M		B	B	B		M		B	M	B		
	Transport								B					
	Health Services												M	
	MBA		M						B					
Applied Science	Computer	B	B			M		B						
	Applied Math	M												
	Chemical Engineering	B												
	Civil Engineering	B												
	Architectural Engineering	M				M								
	Mechanical Engineering	M												
	Environmental							B		B				
	City Planning	B												
	Occupational Safety	B								B				
Education	Special	B								M				
	Administration	B	M											
	Media	B	M											
	Reading					M	B			M				
Other Prof'l	Nursing					M	B		M					
	Recreation Therapy			B										
	Medical Tech.						M							
	Speech Pathology						D				D			
	Criminal Justice		M	B										
	Social Worker								M					
	Interior Decorating													
	Dramatic Arts													M

Art & Science													
Music			B									B	
Art			B										
Psychology		M				B							
General Communication						B							
Liberal Studies							M						
Political Science						B							
Spanish								M					
French								M					
German								M					
Economics				B							B		
Chemistry				B									
Totals	5B 4M	1B 2M	3B 3M	6B	4B	2B 5M	5M 2D	2B 5M	4B	1M 1D	2B	1B 3M	1M

Key: B = BA or BS
MA or MEd or MEng or MSW
D = PhD

that particular campus. Its three graduate programs could also prove to be magnetic, particularly the MBA. The additions at the other four TBIs will strengthen them academically, if funded, but will not give real leverage to desegregation.

Table 5–2 contrasts new degree authorizations for the TBIs with those for the TWIs, as listed in the same *Long Range Plan*. These show plans for thirty-four degree programs, fourteen of them in the same fields as the twenty-nine programs at TBIs. Our concern is not with degree program duplication per se, but with the absence of a policy to limit the expansion of TWIs during a period of equalization and enhancement of TBIs, a period also characterized by declining student numbers! Several high-growth fields also appear on the TWI list, not the TBI: medical technologies, health services management, graduate nursing, and environmental studies are among these entries.

LACK OF EDUCATIONAL INFRASTRUCTURE IN DEGREE PROGRAM OFFERINGS

As we showed in Chapter Three, the TBIs are thin in their undergraduate course offerings, both in the absolute and in comparison with the TWIs. These TBI shortages in course offerings are consequential for the newly approved degree programs that are specified in the consent decree. A review of the new programs against our course analyses suggests that successful implementation will require substantial course additions to provide the infrastructure necessary to effectively support and nurture the new TBI authorization.

For instance, Central currently has only two undergraduate computer science courses, far fewer than at any TWI. To create even a minimally adequate degree program, Central will have to add at least eight courses. This would put its program within competitive range of the offerings at some of the smaller TWIs, but will not allow Central to compare with the depth of computer science offerings at seven of the ten TWIs. The same general observation holds for Elizabeth City, which needs new courses to reach the minimum of ten.

At Fayetteville, the graduate degree in special education will rest on a non-existant undergraduate foundation. This will have negative consequences for recruitment of students and the ultimate viability of the program. The same is true of a new Fayetteville graduate program in educational administration.

Winston-Salem will need to add three courses for its new accounting program just to make the ten needed for a major and put it on a competitive footing with the seven TWIs that offer accounting in significant depth. Assuming that its new general communications degree focuses on journalism and speech and dramatic arts, Winston-Salem will also need to add courses in these areas to bring it up to par with the TWIs that have such courses. This is particularly the case for speech and dramatic arts. The need to develop infrastructure is also evident for Winston-Salem's new Spanish, chemistry, and economics programs. None of these offerings currently reaches the desired minimum of ten, much less the richness and depth evident at the TWIs.

Finally, a new applied math program at Elizabeth City will require substantial course increases if it is to compete with the math offerings evident at even the weakest of the TWIs.

In contrast, the new programs at the TWIs appear to enjoy the support of firm, strong infrastructures of course offerings. For example, the new East Carolina degree in general communications will rest on a foundation of seventeen journalism courses and fifty-six speech and dramatic arts courses (compared to Winston-Salem's five and eleven, respectively). Asheville's new computer science program will build on eight extant courses (compared to Central's two). And, Wilmington's new graduate special education program will rest on its undergraduate offering of six courses (compared to Fayetteville's one).

In sum, thirteen of the twenty-nine new TBI degree programs rest on weak course foundations. Only four of the thirty-four new TWI programs (graduate reading education at Wilmington and Charlotte, undergraduate environmental studies and accounting at Asheville) appear to rest on comparably weak foundations. If the TBIs' new programs—which are the heart of the consent decree—are to take root and flourish, their course foundations must be substantially strengthened as an integral part of the new programs' implementation. The decree does not provide or pledge the additional resources to bring this to pass. Indeed, it does not even commit firmly to implementing these duplicative additions.

EQUALITY OF ACCESS

The consent decree also rests on the premise that Title VI of the Civil Rights Act is fulfilled when prospective college students exercise freedom in choosing where to apply for admission, when they have been affirmatively welcomed through outreach and recruitment, and when on arrival for study they find a reasonably diverse and abundant array of degree programs from which to choose. We call this combination of free choice with abundant program supply the "policy theory" of equality of access. It was rejected long ago by the Supreme Court as insufficient and unworkable for public lower education, but the new UNC/OCR degree asserts that it fits higher education, where attendance is not compulsory.

The rationale used to justify it is based on a serious misuse of the economic analyses introduced into evience by UNC during the trial. It takes the one output of higher education on which those studies, like most economic studies, have focused (i.e., the contribution of schooling to a student's labor market status) and suggests that this is the *only* output of higher education (or at least the only one where equity is a concern). From here, UNC goes on to argue that any determination of equality of access should be focused on the *outcome* of students' educations; that is, educational services per se are not what matters, but rather what employment impact those services have.

This policy theory is objectionable in its witting regression from affirmative action and its rather cynical view of the role of a university. It falls short of comprehensively redistributive justice, which extends from faculty to administration, to trustees, to plant, to the very content of instruction.

We forecast that the theory will have two gravely inequitable effects on UNC campuses by 1990. First, the decree plans to enroll one black student for every white until 4,000 more black students are enrolled at TWIs. If this succeeds, it will greatly reinforce the expansion plans of many of those campuses. Secondly, it will lead to the collapse of two or three of the five TBIs.

The model on which the estimates shown in Table 5–3 are based was tested and illustrates these effects. It is based on the 1979 UNC undergraduate headcount. At that time, the fifteen campuses (School of the Arts was excluded) had 92,489 students. The 1990 mode assumes, in keeping with the decree, a *slight* student growth at East Carolina, Greensboro, Charlotte, and Wilmington because these are places where plans for growth in plant and programs have been in place since 1974. Finally, as a protection against projection bias, it assumes an increase of 914 black students systemwide.

In the model, the decree goal of 11 percent black at TWIs is met and the goal of 15 percent whites at TBIs is nearly met. In addition, the TWIs have 4,330 more black students enrolled than they did in 1990—a close approximation of the 4,000 goal stated in the decree.

Something else happens at the TBIs, however. A&T's enrollment drops from 4,863 in 1979 to 3,400 in 1990. We have depicted Fayetteville as holding steady due to its location and enhancement, but overall as black students have been given increased access to the TWIs, the TBIs have lost 3,416 black students while their white enrollments have remained nearly constant.

Table 5–3
Estimated Effects of the Consent Decree on Undergraduate Desegregation
in 1990

Campus	Total Headcount				% Black
	White	Black	Other	Total	
General Baccalaureate					
TBI					
1) ECSU	100	1,000	70	1,170	85
2) WSSU	200	1,300	30	1,530	85
3) FSU	300	1,700	100	2,100	81
Subtotal	600	4,000	200	4,800	83
TWI					
4) UNC-A	1,800	200	20	2,020	10
5) PSU	1,300	350	500	2,150	16
6) UNC-W	4,000	450	50	4,500	10
Subtotal	7,100	1,000	570	8,670	11
Comprehensive					
TBI					
7) NC/A&T	200	3,000	200	3,400	88
8) NCCU	200	3,000	50	3,250	92
Subtotal	400	6,000	250	6,650	90
TWI					
9) WCU	4,900	400	180	5,480	7
10) UNC-C	7,000	1,600	300	8,900	18
Subtotal	11,900	2,000	480	14,380	14
Doctoral and Other TWIs					
11) ASU	8,000	350	50	8,400	4
12) ECU	10,000	2,050	50	12,100	17
13) UNC-C	6,500	1,600	100	8,200	19
14) NCSU	13,500	1,500	500	15,500	10
15) UNC-Ch	13,000	1,300	300	14,600	9
Subtotal	51,000	6,800	1,000	58,800	11
Total	71,000	19,800	2,500	93,300	21
TWI	70,000	9,800	2,050	81,050	12
TBI	1,000	10,000	450	11,450	87

Admittedly, what materializes in 1990 could be different from our model in some respects. In one respect it will not be, however, and that is in overall black and white undergraduate enrollments. Our model merely illustrates how whites may be expected to continue to choose TWIs and how blacks will choose TWIs in increasing numbers. In the process, A&T will face its demise, shrinking to 70 percent of its present size. Elizabeth City, the least well-developed TBI, will shrink to 77 percent of its present size.

The equality of access policy theory is also based on the theorem that the academically best qualified seek out the best degree program and campus opportunities. Thus, in its implementation, the level of ability of black students at the TBIs will decline inevitably. The process of loss of both enrollment and reputational viability will complete the demise of several TBIs.

The UNC Board of Governors will soon have to choose between two "logical" policy alternatives. The Board can elect to maintain the five TBI campuses as a kind of "lower tier" of colleges where the poorest students, academically and financially, find a credentialing refuge against unemployability. In this event, the Board can celebrate the fruits of its negotiations in the 1981 decree because the TBIs will have 13 to 15 percent whites and plenty of space for programs and facility use.

The only justification for this choice, however, is the cynical view offered by a number of UNC witnesses that, for less able students, obtaining a degree matters much more than what is behind that degree. The true nature of this view is best seen in the logical extension of the argument that what is best for less able black students are *separate and unequal* facilities. It is difficult to imagine for how long the University would continue to endorse such a cynical affront to racial justice.

On the other hand, the Board can expand on its earlier commitment to quality, expressed in its threat to close nursing programs at some TBIs, and can move to discontinue from one to three TBIs. The pressure to do the latter, if population shrinkage and economic slowdown continue, will be enormous. Either option will spell unequal treatment for some of the TBIs. And, either option will be embarrassing in view of degree program expansions at TWIs and TBIs in 1981.

STRATIFICATION OF TBIS

The consent decree continues the stratification of the TBIs at the lowest rungs on the UNC institutional ladder. In essence, the TBIs will continue to hold their stigmatized reputation as havens for those students with weakest academic records or SAT scores who come to college with little preparation and academic ability, most of whom are black students.

The decree accomplishes this by two significant omissions. First, it fails to *consolidate* from TWIs to TBIs the programs that might immediately draw higher-ability students to the latter at the undergraduate level. Second, it makes no provision for increasing, enhancing, and differentiating remedial and support services at TBIs so that they might become magnetically attractive to *both* black and white students who need to overcome educational disadvantagement. Without some sort of consolidation to immediately attract the better students and without magnetization as compensatory entities, the TBIs will continue to be perceived as watered-down, inferior institutions that serve the poorest students.

That this is indeed the image of the TBIs is inherent in a major argument of UNC's case: inferior (black) students are better off among their own kind (at TBIs), for their own good and the good of the educational programs and institutions involved. UNC argues sometimes directly and sometimes by implication that the less academically able student cannot survive in a high-caliber or even "normal" academic program. By restricting UNC's offerings to these levels, access would thus be denied to black students. Further, UNC argued, the educational enterprise would be severely diluted or damaged by the inclusion of these less able students through consequent deflation and cheapening of both program offerings and degrees. Hence, education for the less able should be separate, and transferring TWI programs to TBIs would destroy the programs.

This basic theme and the consent decree that stems from it are directly counter to twenty years of experience in lower education in tracking and isolating the educationally disadvantaged. Research in this area served to show that tracking and isolating poorer students offers no educational advantage and is detrimental socially.[3] On the educational side, subjecting the less able to isolation tends to create a self-fulfilling prophecy among both students and teachers that such students indeed cannot achieve academically. In addition, isolation tends to mean that students receive substantially watered-down courses and programs so that their education is actually inferior.

On the social side, the disadvantaged students are quickly and severely stigmatized by isolative tracking. They are labeled by teachers and peers as "dumb" and generally inferior. (Perhaps even worse, they label themselves accordingly.) Their programs of study are perceived as "the dummies' courses," and are avoided by other students. The effects of such labeling are potent, and serve to perpetuate segregation and isolation. Numerous studies have found that the labels attached in the early elementary years stay with and shape a student.

There is no evidence in studies of either educational practice or human learning to suggest that the research on lower education is not generalizable to higher education. Human learning factors and human social processes and perceptions do not change dramatically at age eighteen. To the contrary, there is evidence in both UNC's arguments and in our analysis of courses that the lower education experience is replicated in higher education at UNC. On the one hand, UNC presents TBIs as homes for those students who would not otherwise be able to attain access. On the other hand, our course analyses clearly establish the general watered-down quality of the TBIs in terms of depth and breadth of course offerings.

There is also evidence of the consent decree's potential for continued stratification in the SAT scores of UNC's entering freshmen. Current SAT score distributions show that low-ability students are found in significant numbers of *all* UNC institutions. Second, the central tendencies of TBI/TWI SAT distributions differ. Not surprisingly, since blacks generally score lower than whites on any standardized test at any grade level and since the TBIs are mostly black, the mean scores for the TBIs are lower than for the TWIs. And naturally, the TBIs have greater proportions of low-SAT freshmen than do the TWIs.[4]

The TBI/TWI overlap in SAT scores reveals that UNC is *already* integrating low- and high-ability students to a substantial degree (and could easily go further in this regard). However, our concern about the stratification potential of the consent decree leads us to focus on the differences in the SAT score distribution.

The point is simple: the TBIs have a larger proportion of students in the lower SAT score ranges than do the TWIs. In other words, there is a pooling of low-scoring black students at the TBIs, and this pooling effect is constant over time.[1] In other words, without powerfully desegregative intervention, low-scoring freshmen (blacks) will continue to pool at the TBIs, and the image of inferior schools for inferior students will be perpetuated.

Continued stigmatization of the TBIs will have significant consequences for equality of access. The TBIs' ability to compete with the reputationally empowered TWIs for a continually diminishing pool of students will be further depressed, contributing yet another force towards the decline and demise of the TBIs.

The degrees granted by TBIs will also be tainted and devalued by their image of inferiority. In the tightening job markets of the 1980s and 1990s, increasing emphasis will be placed on the reputational feature of college degrees. It will *not* be enough to simply have a degree per se. Graduates will need degrees that employers respect. What UNC refuses to recognize is that the apparent value of any degree for blacks found in labor market studies is a temporary phenomenon, resulting from a labor market imbalance that can only persist in the future *if* blacks continue to be denied access to higher education. Thus, even if all the TBIs were to survive, we are forced to ask the ultimate question: equality of access for blacks to what?

RESOURCE ALLOCATIONS

In parallel with the "remedial actions," the consent decree also contains assurances and guarantees on the part of the UNC Board that there will be "equal support" (i.e., funding) across the sixteen campuses. These assurances, however, are put forward within the context of the earlier testimony of UNC Financial Vice President L. Felix Joyner that the most appropriate measure of equal support is "state appropriation and tuition receipts per budgeted full-time equivalent student." In terms of this measure, Joyner's data imply that equality of funding now exists.[5] As a result, the decree amounts to a promise to continue current policies regarding resource allocations. More importantly, the decree will serve as an obstacle to any future relative enhancement of the TBIs (or at least as a rationale for not doing so), since such enhancement, by Joyner's measure, would mean unequal funding.

The consent decree does not move to *enhance* the TBIs by giving them an increased share of UNC's total expenditures for academic purposes, yet it is just such enhancement that is called for in the Revised Criteria prepared for Judge Pratt by OCR in 1978! What the black campuses get under the consent decree is a pledge of *equal* expenditures pegged to enrollments. Thus, declines in TBI enrollments will reduce funding; this will further reduce attractiveness and retention of students, leading to further enrollment declines.

The budgetary actions of the North Carolina General Assembly and the UNC Board of Governors since the signing of the consent decree are completely consistent with this forecast and offer strong support for the likelihood of its accuracy in the future. Faced with severe fiscal constraints in 1981, the General Assembly appropriated considerably less than UNC requested. In fact, the only new system-wide funding approved (i.e., other than the appropriation for continuing operations) was for enrollment growth. And 60 percent of these monies were to be generated by the tuition increases noted earlier.

As Table 5–4 shows, the TBIs (which had been projected for little enrollment growth by the general administration) did not fare well; they received only a small fraction of the amount allocated to their TWI counterparts. Moreover, given the need at the TBIs for additional

Table 5–4
Additional Funds for Current Operations at Selected UNC Campuses, 1981–82

Institutional Group	Total Additional Funds	Additional Funds for Instruction
General Baccalaureate		
TBIs	$ 413 million	$233 million
TWIs	1,204 million	795 million
Comprehensive		
TBIs	277 million	130 million
TWIs	1,338 million	903 million

Source: UNC Board of Governors, 1981–83 Budget *Report and Recommendations.*

administrative and support staff, they received even relatively less of the funds authorized for instructional purposes. The difference in the consequences for program development at the two groups of institutions is striking. The Board of Governors authorized twenty-seven new faculty positions at TWI general baccalaureate campuses and twenty-nine at TWI comprehensive campuses, but only eight and four at their respective TBI counterparts.

The General Assembly also severely cut proposed capital appropriations. Funding was approved only for repairs to walks and roadways, OSHA requirements, building repairs and four new projects (including a regional activity complex at Western Carolina and a recreation complex at Central). Moreover, two-thirds of approved building repairs at the TWIs were to academic buildings, but none of the repairs authorized at the TBIs were to structures used for academic purposes.

A number of statements by members of the General Assembly suggest that this situation (of little or no funding growth) is not likely to change soon. Many members are still committed to giving first priority on any new monies to funding adequate staff salary increases. Moreover, the General Assembly is still on record (since 1978) as committed to an overall student-faculty ratio of 16:1. Given projected enrollment growth and the current 15.5:1 ratio, it could achieve this objective by not funding enrollment growth in either of the next two years.

Some observers already see it as a foregone conclusion that there will be little, if any, new money in 1983. And as each year goes by, the potential benefits from funding the newly authorized programs at the TBIs diminish. Once the TBIs start to decline, the process is difficult to reverse, especially given the existing budgetary system. Currently, UNC is projecting noticeable growth (among the TBIs) only at Fayetteville. In fact, if the 1982 appropriation is repeated next year, the five TBIs combined would receive authorization for only seven or eight new faculty positions.

In addition to the current mood of the General Assembly, 1984 and 1985 are expected to be the years when the full effects of President Reagan's fiscal federalism will first be felt. Given North Carolina's current tax effort for higher education (50 percent above the national average), we cannot expect any real funding growth, especially when additional funds for higher education are not forthcoming in other states. As a result, in the absence of significant, conscious, intercampus redistribution of resources, enhancement of at least some of the TBIs will not be implemented, putting the viability of these institutions into serious question.

There are two important lessons to be drawn from these budget-related developments. One is that proposed substantive remedies for desegregating higher education should recognize the way in which the particular budgetary process involved operates to preserve the status quo. North Carolina is typical—in general, evolutionary change in resource allocations occurs only during times when total resources are expanding. And, proposed remedies must also recognize the way in which the budgetary process operates to mask the subtleties of past discrimination.

EQUAL EDUCATIONAL OPPORTUNITY

The components of the consent decree discussed above will prevent the achievement of equal educational opportunity in North Carolina. The Reagan Administration's acceptance of the University's position regarding the appropriate operational criteria for measuring equality of opportunity and the appropriate means for eliminating any existing inequality represents a significant departure from the case the government presented in court. In particular,

- there is a change in focus from "equality in the provision of educational services" to "equality of access to the University's resources";

- there is abandonment of the position that the viability of the TBIs must be included in consideration of equity; and

- there is, indirectly, a shift from the position that some short-run inefficiency may be necessary to achieve long-run equity, to the view that movement towards greater equity must recognize the need for efficiency in the allocation of resources as an appropriate constraint.

Clearly this is a much narrower interpretation of the requirements of Title VI, although the University and the government assert that they have the same basic objectives.

The data tables originally offered in evidence by Felix Joyner are appended to the consent decree, without comment. While their inclusion is more symbolic than substantive, it gives credence to the view that this decree is a ratification of the status quo. But, more important, it also implies acceptance by the government of UNC's view that the issues in this case—and in achieving the objectives of Title VI in general—are basically a *management* problem that can best be solved by avoiding changes that would "seriously disrupt" the existing system and make it less manageable. In short, they argue that evolutionary change within the existing organizational structure is the only appropriate course.

What we have tried to make clear is not only that such an approach is not the only appropriate one, but also that it won't even work. Its fatal flaw lies in the fact that its success is linked to favorable economic conditions. In a world of expanding opportunities, it is not especially difficult to give a disproportionate share to the previously disadvantaged. But no one is forecasting expanding opportunities in the near future.

Indeed, the real dispute here, which is much more fundamental (and central to any future civil rights progress), is how we should deal with a fixed amount of resources. UNC begins by assuming them away. Its "managerial solution" is grounded in two other arguments. One is that the search for remedies should be based on "access" and "efficiency." It says that blacks are entitled to a share of any resources that are not already committed; that is, the University can only give them a disproportionate share of those resources which are new or in surplus. Second, and probably more important, UNC argues that to effectively manage, it must have control over any changes.

Given the absence of surplus resources, meaningful desegregation can only come by significantly disrupting the existing order. One real tragedy here is that program consolidations, such as those we proposed earlier, would certainly be more cost-effective from a societal perspective (the issue, of course, is *who* benefits and *who* incurs costs) and might well generate the surplus needed to adequately fund many programs. Without such a reallocation, there simply will not be adequate resources in the foreseeable future to fund desegregation.

In Conclusion

Thus, after a decade of dispute and after millions of public dollars' worth of litigation during 1980, the new Reagan Administration accepted a plan that did not meet the criteria for complying with Title VI devised in 1978, that will not desegregate the black campuses, that will increase (from 7 to 10.6 percent) the presence of blacks on some but not all white campuses, and that will damage two or three of the black colleges in a permanent way.

Above all, these changes are *not* obligatory. They are to be carried out to the extent that events appear to be subject to control by the officers of the UNC system: "Significantly altered economic or demographic conditions shall not result in a finding of noncompliance with this Decree, the fourteenth amendment, or Title VI." Above all, the decree gives UNC freedom from OCR challenges and guaranteed absence of the threat of witholding federal funds from 1981 through 1988.

No consent decree can be devoid of some concessions from both parties. Thus UNC has pledged improvements in informational activities and in all forms of outreach to in-state black students. It pledges improvements in the transferability of students from two-year community colleges and in liaison with public high schools. These and the extension of student recruitment efforts may well heighten the four-year college-going rates of North Carolina blacks. Similar pledges for improving access to graduate and professional programs will also have positive effects on enrollment rates.

Extra funds for the two ongoing aid programs for minority presence are *not* pledged, but continuation at current levels is. Thus undergraduate aid amounting to $720,000 per year, and graduate aid of $280,000 per year, will be divided among the colleges for cross-race recruitment. Medical and dental school aid for minorities will also be maintained. So, too, the same old $400,000 a year will go toward doctoral studies for black faculty.

Current operating budgets, student-faculty ratios, faculty salaries, library funds, financial aid for students, and tuition rates are all defined as equal now and pledges are made to keep them equal across campuses. Plants are *being made equal* now through new construction, renovations, and repairs, according to the decree, and equality will be maintained.

The newly authorized degree programs do not have to be established before December 31, 1986. And, if UNC decides that one of the new programs is not needed, it can cancel the plan and come up with something else. If the Board closes down a degree program such as nursing at a TBI, the decree pledges to put the equivalent resources into some other TBI degree program, old or new.

What was "gained," then, by the advent of the decree? The Reagan Administration gained a plan for a *deliberate* effort by UNC to promote cross-race enrollments—not at a rate that will desegregate the campuses, to be sure, but in a way that acknowledges this as a valid goal for the system. (It was so acknowledged in 1974, but that is not very pertinent now.) It also gained a pledge to maintain current levels of funding.

UNC gained a six-year respite from litigation, clinched its control over its own operations, and set aside issues of faculty, administrative, and board member desegregation. It had to authorize some new degree programs, but it does not *have* to fund or establish them. Its only added expenses will come for information dissemination and student recruitment.

We forecast that the net effect of the decree, if the Court of Appeals lets it stand, will be to widen the quality gap between the TWIs and TBIs, to damage seriously the enrollment viability of at least two of the TBIs (A&T and Elizabeth City), and to block the furtherance of Title VI and *Adams* for most of the 1980s. If the issue can be rejoined after 1988, both OCR and UNC will have been discredited as sources of policy design solutions for the problem of attaining racially equal treatment in public colleges and universities.

The case of UNC, in this final analysis, illuminates the clouded corners of higher education in America. The black and white campuses *can* become "just campuses" if those who control them will move to truly enhance the deprived campuses, to eliminate invidious duality, and to equalize academic services across comparable degree programs. These actions can be taken without increased expenses, if the will to change is present. The consent decree's content reveals that this will is missing, whereas the will to preserve a stratified, partially dual, racially identifiable, and unequal set of campuses is very intense. We think this is illuminating because academic preferences for the latter are probably very widely shared, even where *de jure* segregation never existed.

Knowledge and the means for its production and dissemination were extremely *scarce* during most of the years from the founding of Harvard College in 1636 to the G.I. Bill of 1946. Higher education has tended to organize itself around the fact of that scarcity. Academic elitism, campuses arrayed in long tiers of highly stratified quality, and barriers to equal access were expressions of that organizational quest. In the 1960s, we entered a new era of comparative abundance, at the same time that the technology of dissemination has undergone revolutionary change. As we stand poised on the brink of a new and possibly protracted economic depression, the case of UNC reminds us that we can strain to revert to our ancient assumptions about scarcity—some of them rooted in the economics of racial oppression—or we can imagine a future that merges the vision of merit with the vision of equity.

NOTES

1. *North Carolina v. Department of Education.* No. 79-217-CIV-5. Consent Decree, 34.

2. Ibid.; refer also to *North Carolina Populations, June 1980,* office of State Budget and Management, Raleigh, N.C.

3. A. Harry Passow, ed. *Opening Opportunities for Disadvantaged Learn-*

ers, Teachers College Press: New York, 1972, pp. 111–129; Ray C. Rist, *The Urban School: A Factory for Failure,* MIT Press: Cambridge, MA 1973.

4. For more general evidence of the same sort, see Thomas, *Black Students in Higher Education,* pp. 49–74.

5. L. Felix Joyner, *Adams v. Califano,* D.D.C.Civ.A. No. 3095-70, pp. 11,000–12,407.

EPILOGUE

The trial of UNC has thus illuminated the larger issue of the purposes of public higher education. It has done this on the threshold of a decade of declining enrollments, declining state funding, and now, reduced federal aid.

No regime can be held accountable for many of the contraditions that grew up out of policies developed across a variety of issues; but in this instance the Reagan Administration has enabled UNC to continue to qualify for federal aid without acting to eliminate racial barriers left from the past. It has also embraced the idea of aid to stimulate cross-race enrollments, while it has moved to slash its own aid in its budget proposals. In February 1982, the White House budget sent to the Congress contained a $2.2 billion cut in federal money for student aid, to begin in the fall of 1982. Education Secretary Bell termed the 1980–1981 funding an unaffordably "posh" student aid program.

Lincoln University President Herman Branson said the cuts would spell "disaster for us." Robert Stevens, President of Haverford College, argued that *even* middle-class students would be hurt. The American Council on Education estimated that 700,000 students now receiving federally guaranteed aid will become ineligible. Wesleyan University became the first of a series of colleges to announce formal termination of its "need-blind" admissions policy, turning instead to admission based on ability to pay tuition, among other criteria, of course.[1]

Even though the Congress revamped the aid proposal, its advent suggests one of two logical inferences: the consent decree was aimed at the withdrawal of concern over federal enforcement of Title VI, or it meant this concern was combined with no awareness of the

133

critically essential role of federal aid in equalizing higher educational opportunity.

The issue of purposes served by the consent decree is opened by the question of minority access, but when we enter the corridor of policy options we see that they go beyond the matter of racial injustice to include the matter of who shall be admitted and who shall be helped in the study of what subjects and skills. The 1960s began to make of public colleges an exceptionally inclusive and hospitable network of campuses and degree programs. Public higher education began to approximate a relatively free and increasingly universal extension of public lower education. The trial and the consent decree of UNC show that this development has been impeded severely during the 1980s and perhaps long after.

Under the emerging policy pattern, state university systems in perhaps forty out of fifty states will soon come to be defined as "overbuilt." Less prestigious campuses will be shut down or swallowed up by the larger campuses. The ideal of designing instruction to guide, equalize, and facilitate learning, through remedial, compensatory, and diversified approaches, may give way to a reversion to the ideal of heightened selectivity based on indicators of student rankings on tests and high school grades. Graduate study in the liberal arts will continue to decline as opportunities for faculty appointments diminish.

Little attention may be paid in the midst of these trends to the fact that, with diminished resources and uneven competition, some campuses will survive to produce graduates whose B.A.s and B.S.s are demonstrably—indeed, more and more grossly—inferior to the degrees of sister institutions within the same state systems. The evaluative sifting function—labor screening—of public colleges will become the dominant purpose of the higher learning. The rationale for admitting only the highest-ranking high school graduates, except on very inferior campuses, may be restored to the place it enjoyed in some states before World War II.

Blacks, Puerto Ricans, Chicanos, and Native Americans, all of whom now get the worst of it from the educational process, will lose their brief era of entitlement to an extra opportunity. Minority aid funds will dry up as federal aid diminishes. The battle between aid based on need and aid based on test scores will be renewed, and elitism will triumph. As the fate of these ethnic minorities dims in public higher education, the fate of large numbers of poor and working-class whites will be dimmed in corresponding degree.

This is not the trend Governor James Hunt, the Board of Governors of UNC, or UNC President William Friday sought to bring about in their litigation or in the decree. The UNC plans are plainly more inclusive and hospitable than the future we have outlined will become. What they accomplished, however, was the identification of common ground between the regressive and punitive policy aims of Senator Jesse Helms, leading both the state party and a vital segment of the Reagan Administration, and the UNC leadership. That common ground comprises a renewed celebration of academic elitism. If that value preference carries in its wake the contemporary equivalent of Social Darwinism, this will seem to be due to events beyond the control of the state university. It will be deemed the fault of the economy and demography.

All of these trends are captured, expressed, and reinforced by the consent decree. The decree is the result of political collaboration between UNC, Senator Helms and the Reagan Administration. Creative as that collaboration appears to be, it fails to include the U.S. Court of Appeals. We have been told that its eleven members are quite evenly divided between those who intend to guard the decision reached in *Adams v. Richardson,* a decision we believe has been evaded by the decree, and those who want a new opportunity to limit the distance travelled by Judge Pratt in that landmark decision.

The principle of separation of powers will once again be called upon to test the rights of black Americans. If the consent decree is invalidated or even remanded for reconsideration by the Court of Appeals, we can conclude that this constitutional principle continues to be the best refuge for racial minorities in search of equality. If the consent decree is upheld, we can expect some long years of renewed indifference and discrimination in higher education.

Indeed, rehearing the case will be fraught with dangers. For example, the government and Morgan Associates have already joined in co-preparing for the new hearing. They can reconcile their arguments and meld their representations of facts; they can also stand upon and shore up the reasoning of the earlier two appelate judges who found that Judge Dupree had jurisdiction and exercised it with procedural correctness. Rauh and the LDF will be further isolated, deprived of support from OCR. In addition, if the Appeals Court again supports Dupree and therefore the consent decree, a choice will face LDF about whether to try the Supreme Court.

If they do try, and if that body affirms the decree or, more problematically, challenges the *Adams* decision, the edifice begun by Title VI will begin to crumble nationwide. Lawyers call this the possibility of "making bad law." We are in a political era when the foundation of civil rights, resting upon *Brown*, could crack open. The *substance* of the consent decree and its dubious origins may never get a real chance for scrutiny. Alternatively, there may well be five appellate judges as willing and as able as Skelly Wright was to see through the facade of the decree. Six votes will suffice.

This trial will be resumed during 1983. The legal precedents for bringing into being an equal and educationally responsive form of higher education were too well established between 1930 and 1973 to be neglected for long. Perhaps by 1990, the Legal Defense Fund will not have to stand alone. Perhaps, next time it will be joined by portions of the higher education community itself.

Note

1. *New York Times*, February 16, 1982, A–1, B–8.

APPENDICES

There are a few tables scattered through the text of this book, but the great bulk of statistical evidence on which our reasoning is based is contained in these Appendices, which are organized as follows:

Appendix A contains the student enrollment and staffing data fundamental to Chapter Two. Tables A–1 through A–8 present evidence pertinent to segregation. Tables A–9 through A–13 present evidence pertinent to a model for desegregating the UNC campuses.

Appendix B contains the data on degree programs, courses of study, and SAT scores fundamental to Chapter Three. Tables B–1 through B–7 present evidence on degree and course differences. Tables B–8 through B–13 present evidence on SAT score differences.

Appendix C contains financial data fundamental to Chapter Four.

APPENDIX A

Data on Student Enrollment and Staffing

Table A–1
1979 UNC Undergraduate Enrollments by Campus and Race

| Campus | | Total Headcount | | | | % Black |
		White	Black	Other	Total	
General Baccalaureate						
TBI						
1) ECSU		162	1,342	20	1,524	88
2) WSSU		270	1,941	13	2,224	87
3) FSU		213	2,008	60	2,281	88
	Subtotal	645	5,291	93	6,029	88
TWI						
4) UNC-A		1,785	82	26	1,893	4
5) PSU		1,365	238	499	2,102	11
6) UNC-W		3,850	234	48	4,132	6
	Subtotal	7,000	554	573	8,127	7
Comprehensive						
TBI						
7) NC/A&T		198	4,463	202	4,863	92
8) NCCU		286	3,662	62	4,010	91
	Subtotal	484	8,125	264	8,873	92
TWI						
9) WCU		4,907	261	182	5,350	5
10) UNC-C		6,835	569	299	7,703	7
	Subtotal	11,742	830	481	13,053	6
Doctoral and Other						
TWI						
11) ASU		8,029	183	65	8,277	2
12) ECU		9,667	1,049	108	10,824	10
13) UNC-G		6,308	754	81	7,143	11
14) NCSU		13,972	980	573	15,525	6
15) UNC-Ch		13,240	1,120	278	14,638	8
	Subtotal	51,216	4,086	1,105	56,407	7
	Total	71,087	18,886	2,516	92,489	20

Source: DBS Vol. 7, July 10, 1980, pp. 50–58.

Table A–2
1979 UNC Graduate and Professional Enrollments by Campus and Race

Campus	White	Black	Other	Total	% Black
		Total Headcount			
General Baccalaureate					
TBI					
1) ECSU					
2) WSSU					
3) FSU					
Subtotal	——	——	——	——	—
TWI					
4) UNC-A					
5) PSU	101	12	16	129	9
6) UNC-W	111	14	1	126	11
Subtotal	212	26	17	255	10
Comprehensive					
TBI					
7) NC/A&T	139	369	36	544	68
8) NCCU	225	661	21	907	73
Subtotal	364	1,030	57	1,451	71
TWI					
9) WCU	883	21	20	924	2
10) UNC-C	1,064	157	21	1,242	13
Subtotal	1,947	178	41	2,166	8
Doctoral and Other					
TWI					
11) ASU	924	25	16	965	3
12) ECU	1,806	223	21	2,050	11
13) UNC-G	2,515	216	51	2,782	8
14) NCSU	3,118	220	653	3,991	6
15) UNC-Ch	5,417	411	318	6,146	7
Subtotal	13,780	1,095	1,059	15,934	7
Total	16,330	2,329	1,174	19,806	12

Source: DBS Vol. 7, July 10, 1980, pp. 82–120.

Bachelors Degrees by Field—by Campus

Campus Category & Undergraduate Enrollment General Baccalaureate (000–0000)	Education	Business & Management	Social Sciences	Health Professions	Psychology	Public Affairs	Biological Sciences	Architecture & Engineering	Letters	Physical Sciences	Home Economics	Math Science & Computer Science	Fine Arts	Foreign Languages	Agriculture	Interdisciplinary	Degree Totals by University
TBI																	
Elizabeth City (ECSU)	143	63	39	—	—	—	17	—	15	4	—	9	—	—	—	—	290
Winston-Salem (WSSU)	143	75	52	52	20	—	14	—	9	—	—	—	7	—	—	10	382
Fayetteville (FSU)	178	93	109	—	20	—	6	—	8	5	—	8	1	—	—	—	428
Subtotal TBI	464	231	200	52	40	—	37	—	32	9	—	17	8	—	—	10	1100
/Degrees Earned Subtotal TBI	42%	21%	18%	5%	4%	0%	3%	0%	3%	1%	0%	1%	1%	0%	0%	1%	100%
TWI																	
Asheville (UNC-A)	—	39	40	—	28	—	13	—	10	3	—	1	12	16	—	—	170
Pembroke (FSU)	155	41	124	—	22	—	23	—	18	5	10	11	2	1	—	—	412

Degrees Earned

Table A–3 continued

	Education	Business & Management	Social Sciences	Health Professions	Psychology	Public Affairs	Biological Sciences	Architecture & Engineering	Letters	Physical Sciences	Home Economics	Math Science & Computer Science	Fine Arts	Foreign Languages	Agriculture	Interdisciplinary	Degree Totals by University
							Degrees Earned										
Wilmington (UNC-W)	117	74	100	11	27	—	82	—	37	33	—	14	13	2	—	12	522
Subtotal TWI	272	154	272	11	77	—	118	—	65	41	10	26	27	19	—	12	1104
/Degrees Earned Subtotal TWI	25%	14%	25%	1%	7%	0%	11%	0%	6%	4%	1%	2%	2%	2%	0%	1%	100%
Total General Baccalaureate	736	385	472	63	117	—	155	—	97	50	10	43	35	19	—	22	2204
/Degrees Earned General BA.	33%	18%	21%	3%	5%	0%	7%	0%	4%	2%	1%	2%	2%	1%	0%	1%	100%
Comprehensive (3400–5700) TBI																	
A and T (NCA & T)	107	139	42	56	35	47	23	81	.17	5	38	9	8	—	24	1	632
Central (WCCU)	126	167	119	37	31	57	27	—	8	10	38	8	14	5	—	—	647
Subtotal TBI	233	306	161	93	66	104	50	81	25	15	76	17	22	5	24	1	1279
/Degrees Earned Subtotal TBI	18%	24%	13%	7%	5%	8%	4%	6%	2%	1%	6%	1%	2%	.5%	2%	.5%	100%

TWI																
Western Carolina (WCU)	266	190	58	75	29	92	16	—	13	17	29	20	19	5	—	—	829
Charlotte (UNC-C)	100	294	201	101	119	81	51	159	84	37	—	26	24	9	—	—	1286
Subtotal TWI	366	484	259	176	148	173	67	159	97	54	29	46	43	14	—	—	2115
/Degrees Earned Subtotal TWI	17%	23%	12%	8%	7%	8%	3%	8%	5%	3%	1%	2%	2%	1%	0%	0%	100%
Total Comprehensive	599	790	420	269	114	217	117	240	122	69	105	63	63	19	24	1	3394
/Degrees Earned Comprehensive	18%	23%	12%	8%	6%	8%	4%	7%	4%	2%	3%	2%	2%	1%	1%	0%	100%
Grand Total	1335	1175	892	322	331	277	273	240	215	219	115	106	100	38	24	23	5598
/Degrees Earned Grand Totals	24%	21%	16%	6%	6%	5%	5%	4%	4%	2%	2%	2%	2%	1%	.5%	.5%	100%

Source: DBS Vol. 19; July 1980, pp. 365–412.

Table A–4
Full-Time Faculty by Campus and Race, 1979

Campus		White	Black	Other	Total	% Black
				Race		
General Baccalaureate						
TBI						
1) ECSU		21	62	9	92	67
2) WSSU		47	92	6	145	63
3) FSU		45	90	14	149	60
	Subtotal	113	244	29	386	63
TWI						
4) UNC-A		75	0	2	77	0
5) PSU		108	2	12	122	2
6) UNC-W		193	9	6	208	4
	Subtotal	376	11	20	407	2
Comprehensive						
TBI						
7) NC/A&T		68	204	9	281	73
8) NCCU		71	117	6	194	60
	Subtotal	139	321	15	475	68
TWI						
9) WCU		305	0	6	311	0
10) UNC-C		354	18	15	387	5
	Subtotal	659	18	21	698	3
Doctoral and Other						
TWI						
11) ASU		492	6	6	504	1
12) ECU		610	14	15	639	2
13) UNC-G		501	10	5	516	2
14) NCSU		1,108	27	36	1,171	2
15) UNC-Ch		1,627	55	54	1,736	3
	Subtotal	4,338	112	116	4,566	2
	Total	5,625	706	201	6,532	11

Source: DBS Vol. 8, July 9, 1980, pp. 1–20.

Table A–5
Changes in Full-Time Faculty Over Time[1]

Year	15 UNC Campuses			10 TWI Campuses			5 TBI Campuses		
	Black	Total	% Black	Black	Total	% Black	White	Total	% White
1975	661	6,016	10.9	122	5,196	2.3	281	820	34.3
1976	694	6,024	11.5	116	5,160	2.2	286	864	33.1
1977	716	6,338	11.3	114	5,420	2.1	316	918	34.4
1978	693	6,537	10.6	130	5,689	2.3	285	848	33.6
1979	706	6,532	10.8	141	5,671	2.5	296	861	34.4
1980	723	6,603	10.9	148	5,692	2.6	336	911	36.9
1981	740	6,674	11.1	155	5,713	2.7	376	961	39.0
1982	757	6,746	11.2	162	5,734	2.8	417	1,012	41.2
1983	774	6,815	11.4	170	5,793	2.9	418	1,022	40.9
2041			15.0						
2083						10.0			

[1]Data for 1975 through 1979 from *DBS Vol. 8*, July 9, 1980, pp. 1–20. Data for 1980 through 1983 represent projections from rates of change in 1975–1979, using 1983 total based on *UNC Long-Range Plan, 1978–83*, student projections. Assuming no change in subsequent size, and no new remedial actions, total % black faculty would reach 15% in 2041, and 10% at TWI campuses in 2083.

Table A–6
Median Salaries of UNC Faculty by Campus

Campus		1977 Median Salary	1979 Median Salary	1979 ÷ 1977
General Baccalaureate				
TBI				
1) ECSU		$15,232	$18,081	119
2) WSSU		14,768	17,643	119
3) FSU		15,150	17,680	117
	Subtotal (3)	15,050	17,801	118
TWI				
4) UNC-A		$16,782	$19,232	115
5) PSU		15,840	18,927	119
6) UNC-W		15,814	18,703	118
	Subtotal (3)	16,145	18,954	117
Comprehensive				
TBI				
7) NC/A&T		$16,719	$19,785	118
8) NCCU		16,329	19,173	117
	Subtotal (2)	16,524	19,479	118
TWI				
9) WCU		$16,359	$18,875	115
10) UNC-C		15,798	18,316	116
	Subtotal (2)	16,079	18,596	116
Doctoral and Other TWI				
11) ASU		$16,889	$18,972	112
12) ECU		17,553	20,000	114
13) UNC-G		18,261	20,068	110
14) NCSU		20,369	21,953	108
15) UNC-Ch		21,689	28,659	132
	Subtotal (5)	18,952	21,930	114
	Total (15)	$16,903	$19,738	117

Source: Equal Employment Opportunity Commission Higher Education Staff Information Report (EEO-6)

able A–7

79 Administrators by Campus and Race

mpus		White	Black	Other	Total	% Black
			Total Headcount			
neral Baccalaureate						
TBI						
) ECSU		2	26	0	28	93
) WSSU		1	24	0	25	96
) FSU		2	27	1	30	90
	Subtotal	5	77	1	83	93
TWI						
) UNC-A		21	2	1	24	8
) PSU		15	1	7	23	4
) UNC-W		27	1	0	28	4
	Subtotal	63	4	8	75	5
mprehensive						
TBI						
) NC/A&T		1	43	0	44	98
) NCCU		4	38	1	43	88
	Subtotal	5	81	1	87	93
TWI						
) WCU		56	1	0	57	2
) UNC-C		79	2	0	81	2
	Subtotal	135	3	0	138	2
octoral and Other						
TWI						
) ASU		39	0	1	40	0
) ECU		121	5	0	126	4
) UNC-G		85	4	0	89	4
) NCSU		162	6	4	172	3
) UNC-Ch		362	15	5	382	4
	Subtotal	769	30	10	809	4
	Total	977	195	20	1,192	16

urce: DBS Vol. 8, July 9, 1980, pp. 201–216.

Table A-8
Administrative Personnel Changes Over Time[1]

Year	15 UNC Campuses			10 TWI Campuses			5 TBI Campuses		
	Black	Total	% Black	Black	Total	% Black	White	Total	% White
1975	232	1,222	19.0	27	988	2.7	25	234	10.6
1976	205	1,192	17.2	28	992	2.8	21	200	10.5
1977	196	1,114	17.6	27	926	2.9	17	188	9.0
1978	202	1,263	16.0	36	1,083	3.3	12	180	6.7
1979	195	1,192	16.4	37	1,022	3.6	10	170	5.9
1980	207	1,204	17.2	39	1,035	3.8	1	169	0.6
1981	209	1,216	17.2	41	1,043	3.9	5	173	2.9
1982	209	1,228	17.0	42	1,050	4.0	11	178	6.2
1983	213	1,240	17.2	44	1,058	4.2	13	182	7.1
1984	226	1,253	18.0	47	1,077	4.4	3	176	1.7
2010						10.0			

[1]Data for 1975 through 1979 from DBS Vol. 8, July 9, 1980, pp. 201–211. Projections for 1980–1983 assume total personnel based on Long-Range Plan, 1978–1983, student projections, plus rates of change by race characteristic of 1975–1979 period.

ble A–9
ynamic Model of Undergraduate Desegregation

mpus		White	Black	Other	Total	% Black
			Total Headcount			
neral Baccalaureate						
TBI						
) ECSU		828	886	23	1,737	51
) WSSU		1,147	1,215	20	2,382	51
) FSU		1,111	1,229	70	2,410	51
	Subtotal	3,086	3,330	113	6,529	51
TWI						
) UNC-A		1,588	242	30	1,860	13
) PSU		1,377	494	600	2,471	20
) UNC-W		3,470	888	80	4,438	20
	Subtotal	6,435	1,624	710	8,769	19
mprehensive						
TBI						
) NC/A&T		2,281	2,604	220	5,105	51
) NCCU		2,120	2,290	80	4,490	51
	Subtotal	4,401	4,894	300	9,595	51
TWI						
) WCU		5,132	797	200	6,129	13
) UNC-C		6,360	1,690	400	8,450	20
	Subtotal	11,492	2,487	600	14,579	17
octoral and Other						
TWI						
) ASU		7,291	1,101	80	8,472	13
) ECU		8,486	2,570	120	11,176	23
) UNC-G		5,884	1,662	100	7,556	22
) NCSU		11,510	4,090	650	16,250	25
) UNC-Ch		11,000	3,363	300	14,663	23
	Subtotal	44,171	12,786	1,250	58,207	22
	Total	69,585	25,121	2,973	97,679	26

ote: See Table 1 for Data Base, and *UNC Long-Range Plan, 1978–1983*, p. 155.

Table A–10
Undergraduate Program Consolidation

	Major Program of Study								
	Early Childhood	Special Education	Nursing	Medical Records Technology	Law Enforcement, Criminal Justice, Correc. Police Science	Public Administration	Environmental Science & Ecology	Public Communications	Transport Engineering
General Baccalaureate									
TBI									
1) ECSU	CX	X		X	X		X		
2) WSSU	C		CX	CX	CX				
3) FSU		X		CX	CX				C
TWI									
4) UNC-A									
5) PSU			X			X			
6) UNC-W			CX	X	X		CX		
Comprehensive									
TBI									
7) NC/A&T	X	X					CX		
8) NCCU		C			CX	CX			
TWI									
9) WCU		X	X	X	CX			C	X
10) UNC-C			X		X			X	

Doctoral and Other TWI							
11) ASU	CX			X		X	X
12) UNC-G		X	X		X		X
13) ECU	X	CX	CX	CX	X		X
14) NCSU	X		X	X	X		
15) UNC-Ch		CX		X	X	X	X

Notes:
1. C = Consolidate degree program on this campus
   X = Current course offerings of 5 or more
2. Additional, not shown: Arts & Sciences at College of the Albemarle relocated to ECSU. Sciences and Social Sciences at School of the Arts relocated to WSSU.

Table A–11
Dynamic Model of Graduate and Professional Desegregation

Campus		White	Black	Other	Total	% Black
		Total Headcount				
General Baccalaureate						
TBI						
1) ECSU						
2) WSSU						
3) FSU						
	Subtotal	——	——	——	——	—
TWI						
4) UNC-A						
5) PSU						
6) UNC-W						
	Subtotal	——	——	——	——	—
Comprehensive						
TBI						
7) NC/A&T		320	240	40	600	40
8) NCCU		805	600	25	1,505	40
	Subtotal	1,125	840	65	2,035	40
TWI						
9) WCU		790	90	20	900	10
10) UNC-C		1,080	200	20	1,300	15
	Subtotal	1,870	290	40	2,200	13
Doctoral and Other						
TWI						
11) ASU		795	90	15	900	10
12) ECU		1,730	440	30	2,200	20
13) UNC-G		1,880	480	40	2,400	20
14) NCSU		2,440	760	600	3,800	20
15) UNC-Ch		4,580	1,120	300	6,000	19
	Subtotal	11,425	2,890	985	15,300	19
	Total	14,420	4,020	1,090	19,530	20

Source: See Table 2, and *UNC Long-Range Plan*, p. 155.

ble A–12
ynamic Model of Faculty Desegregation

mpus		White	Black	Other	Total	% Black
			Full Time Faculty			
neral Baccalaureate						
TBI						
) ECSU		40	50	10	100	50
) WSSU		75	85	10	170	50
) FSU		75	90	15	180	50
	Subtotal	190	225	35	450	50
TWI						
) UNC-A		69	6	5	80	8
) PSU		105	10	15	130	8
) UNC-W		188	22	10	220	10
	Subtotal	362	38	30	430	9
mprehensive						
TBI						
) NC/A&T		145	155	10	310	50
) NCCU		140	150	10	300	50
	Subtotal	285	305	20	610	50
TWI						
) WCU		314	28	8	350	8
) UNC-C		362	43	20	425	10
	Subtotal	676	71	28	775	9
ctoral and Other						
TWI						
) ASU		480	42	8	530	8
) ECU		595	60	15	670	9
) UNC-G		488	49	8	545	9
) NCSU		971	99	30	1,100	9
) UNC-Ch		1,502	153	45	1,700	9
	Subtotal	4,036	403	106	4,545	9
	Total	5,549	1,042	219	6,810	15

urce: See Tables 4 and 10.

Table A–13
Dynamic Model of Administrative Desegregation

Campus		White	Black	Other	Total	% Black
General Baccalaureate						
TBI						
1) ECSU		15	16	0	31	50
2) WSSU		15	15	0	30	50
3) FSU		17	18	1	36	50
	Subtotal	47	49	1	97	50
TWI						
4) UNC-A		21	3	1	25	10
5) PSU		13	4	8	25	15
6) UNC-W		25	6	0	31	20
	Subtotal	59	13	9	81	16
Comprehensive						
TBI						
7) NC/A&T		23	23	0	46	50
8) NCCU		24	25	1	50	50
	Subtotal	47	48	1	96	50
TWI						
9) WCU		60	6	0	63	10
10) UNC-C		70	17	1	87	20
	Subtotal	130	23	0	150	15
Doctoral and Other						
TWI						
11) ASU		39	5	1	45	10
12) ECU		111	20	0	131	15
13) UNC-G		82	14	0	96	15
14) NCSU		144	24	4	172	14
15) UNC-Ch		324	53	5	382	14
	Subtotal	700	116	10	826	14
	Total	983	249	21	1,253	20

Data Source: See Table 7 and 10.

Data on Degree Programs, Courses of Study, and SAT Scores

Table B–1
Major Rules Guiding Course Counts and Their Rationale

Rule	Rationale
1. Hyphenated courses (e.g., Roman History 101–102) are counted as one single course.	1. Such courses are listed on a single line in the catalog. Counting as one speeds the count and avoids introducing complexity in the counting, thereby reducing chances of error.
2. Sequence courses (e.g., Roman History I & II) are counted as individual courses.	2. Such courses are listed on separate lines in the catalogs, and sometimes are spread throughout a subject area listing rather than grouped together. Counting them as individual courses speeds the counts and avoids introducing complexity in counting, thereby reducing chances of error.
3. Double-lined courses are generally counted as many times as they appear.	3. Speeds the count and avoids introducing complexity, thereby reducing chances of error.
4. Special content courses (e.g., math for teachers) are generally counted under the special area (e.g., education) rather than the content area (e.g., math).	4. Reflects richness in the special area.
5. Biological (and sometimes physical) science courses were sometimes collapsed under a main header (e.g., biology) and sometimes spread out (e.g., biology, anatomy, etc.)	5. Attempts to present each individual institution in the most favorable possible light in order to give UNC the benefit of the doubt. The decision as to whether to collapse or not collapse was made individually for each institution, depending on its array of courses. Where spreading the courses suggested a pitifully thin offering in a major field (e.g., one course here, one course there in the biological sciences), we collapsed (e.g., all under biology). This seemed to us to most favorably reflect the institution's apparent capacity to offer a *general* array of courses in a particular field, but no richness in subspecialities. Where institutions had some notable depth (e.g., several courses across several subjects in a field), we tried to show this by spreading them out.
6. ROTC and non-credit courses are not to be counted.	6. Not essential to degree programs.
7. No distinctions to be made among course levels (remedial, undergraduate, etc.); teaching methods (lab, lecture, etc.); courses of different credit value	7. Speeds the count and avoids introducing complexity, thereby reducing chances of error.

Table B–2
Recount Rule Changes and Their Degree of Impact on the Data

Rule Change	Degree of Impact on Data
1. Sequence courses (e.g., Roman History I and II, with II described as a continuation of I) are counted as one course in the recount.	1. Significant throughout the table. Affects total numbers of courses.
2. Performance courses are excluded from music in the recount.	2. Significant, but only for the category music. Affects total number of courses for music.
3. Double-listed courses are counted only where they first appear in the catalog in the recount.	3. Minor. There are very few double-listings overall. Affects both total numbers and classifications of courses where this occurs.
4. Special content courses (e.g., mathematics for secondary school teachers) are counted under the content area in the recount.*	4. Moderate, but primarily for education and certain related content areas such as music, art, English literature. Affects both total numbers and classifications of courses where this occurs.
5. Biological (and, where appropriate, physical) science courses were spread across subjects in the recount. In the original, these courses were generally collapsed or spread, depending on the depth and breadth of offerings at each individual institution. The judgment to do this was made by each coder.	5. Significant, but only for biological and physical sciences. Affects classification of courses primarily.

*Excepting information systems courses whose titles include specific mention of business, commerce, or marketing, which are counted under the business information systems heading.

Table B–3
Summary of Business and Commerce Offerings (See Table B–4 for more complete information.)

Campus	# Courses	Institution's Concentration of Courses (as % of # courses)*	Distribution of Business Ed, Dist. Ed, Office Admin. (as % of # courses)	
			N	%
General Baccalaureate (900–3000)				
TBI				
ECSU	42	69% MM/ACC.	7	17%
WSSU	39	62% MM/Bus. Ed., etc.	10	26%
FSU	61	67% MM/Bus. Ed., etc.	16	26%
TWI				
UNC-A	29	52% MM	0	0
PSU	34	38% MM	7	21
UNC-W	41	71% MM/Acc.	1	—
ST	246	—	41	—
% at TBI's	58%	—	81%	—
Comprehensive (3400–5700)				
TBI				
NCA & T	55	56% MM/Bus. Ed., etc.	13	24%
NCCU	89	58% Finance & Bank/Bus. Ed., etc.	23	26%
TWI				
WCU	111	63% MM/Bus. Ed., etc.	16	14%
UNC-C	37	73% MM/Acc.	1	—
ST	292	—	53	—
% at TBI's	49%	—	68%	—
Doctoral and Other (6000–13,200)				
TWI Only				
ASU	106	48% MM/Bus. Ed., etc.	19	18%
UNC-G	63	57% MM/Bus. Ed., etc.	17	27%
ECU	73	64% MM/Bus. Ed., etc.	28	38%
NCSU	66	68% MM	1	—
UNC-CH	55	73% MM/Acc.	1	—
ST	363	—	66%	—
Grand Total	901	—	160	—
% Grand Total at TBI's	32%	—	43%	—

*Includes the top two categories over 10. If only one category is ≥ 10, then only that categor
is included.

Number of Undergraduate Courses—Social Sciences

Campus Category & Undergraduate Enrollment	Business & Commerce						Education										
	Management & Marketing	Accounting	Finance & Banking	Insurance & Real Estate	Business Education, Distrib. Education & Office Administration	Other, Information Systems & Health Care Management	Administration & Supervision	Counselor Education	Education Media & Library Science	Elementary	Secondary	Reading	Special Education	Higher Education	Speech Pathology & Audiology	Physical Education & Health	Bilingual Education
General Baccalaureate (900–3000)																	
TBI																	
Elizabeth City (ECSU)	19	10	4	1	7	1		3	11	7	10	12	1		5	34	
Winston-Salem (WSSU)	14	7	3	1	10	4		1	1	3	4	5	9			35	
Fayetteville (FSU)	25	12	4	2	16	2		3	1	1	5	3	1			58	
Subtotal TBI	58	29	11	4	33	7		7	13	11	19	20	11		5	127	
TWI																	
Asheville (UNC-A)	15	1	4	4		5			3	6	3	3				20	
Pembroke (PSU)	13	8	4		7	2		3	7	12	16	15	16		1	32	
Wilmington (UNC-W)	17	12	5	2	1	4			4	7	2	3	6			43	

Table B–4 continued

Campus Category & Undergraduate Enrollment	Business & Commerce						Education											
	Management & Marketing	Accounting	Finance & Banking	Insurance & Real Estate	Business Education, Distrib. Education & Office Administration	Other, Information Systems & Health Care Management	Administration & Supervision	Counselor Education	Education Media & Library Science	Elementary	Secondary	Reading	Special Education	Higher Education	Speech Pathology & Audiology	Physical Education & Health	Bilingual Education
Subtotal TWI	45	21	14	6	8	11		3	14	25	21	21	22		1	95	
Total General Baccalaureate	103	50	24	10	41	18		10	27	36	40	41	33		6	222	
Comprehensive (3400–3700)																	
TBI																	
A and T (NCA & T)	18	12	7	2	13	3		5	13		13	8	7	7	4	73	
Central (NCCU)	18	14	29		23	5	5	1	4	4	4	5	4	1	5	60	
Subtotal TBI	36	26	36	2	36	8	5	6	17	4	17	13	11	8	9	133	
TWI																	
Western Carolina (WCU)	54	13	10	6	16	12	1	4	18	16	12	9	23		10	73	
Charlotte (UNC-C)	17	10	4	2	1	3			7	3	8					39	
Subtotal TWI	71	23	14	8	17	15	1	4	25	19	20	9	23		10	112	
Total Comprehensive	107	49	50	10	53	23	6	10	42	23	37	22	34	8	19	245	

	Doctoral & Other (6000–13,200) TWI Only															
Appalachian State (ASU)		32	15	12	15	19	13	10	19	31	31	13	21	24	19	100
Greensboro (UNC-G)		19	9	5	4	17	9	2	2	8	7	8	3	5		27	191
Eastern Carolina (ECU)		19	12	8	4	28	2	13	2	16	24	23	6	5			153
State (NCSU)		45	5	6	1	1	8		9	4	2	7	5	11	5	8	56
Chapel Hill (UNC-CH)	1	29	11	5	6	1	3		1	15	2	13		4		19	74
Total Other	1	144	52	36	30	66	35	15	24	62	66	82	27	46	29	73	574
Grand Total	1	354	151	110	50	160	78	21	44	131	125	159	90	113	37	90	1041

[1]Catalogs used are those current as of spring/summer 1980 for the 1980–81 academic year.

Table B-4 Continued

Campus Category & Undergraduate Enrollment	Education						Home Economics									
	Early Childhood	Occupational Education	Education Other	Anthropology	Economics	Geography	Clothing & Textiles	Food & Nutrition	Home Management & Child Development	Home Economics Education	History	Political Science	Psychology	Criminal Justice, Law Enforcement, & Police Science	Social Work	Sociology
General Baccalaureate (900–3000)																
TBI																
Elizabeth City (ECSU)	6	3	23	2	8	4					23	18	15	14	8	18
Winston-Salem (WSSU)	5		6	4	8	5			1		33	36	16	25	5	16
Fayetteville (FSU)	2		6	6	19	22					42	33	24	39	18	16
Subtotal TBI	13	3	35	12	35	31			1		98	87	55	78	18	50
TWI																
Asheville (UNC-A)	2		8	5	18	1					28	23	38	3		27
Pembroke (PSU)			15		10	12	4	6	12	4	15	46	33	8	9	29
Wilmington (UNC-W)	8		16	23	18	14					48	31	36	10	8	30

Subtotal TWI	10	3	39	28	46	27	4	6	12	4	91	107	100	21	17	86
Total General Baccalaureate	23	3	74	34	81	58	4	6	13	4	189	162	187	60	35	136
Comprehensive (3400–5700)																
TBI																
A and T (NCA & T)	9	35	41	2	32	9	5	23	25	7	49	39	27		13	28
Central (NCCU)			20	1	26	23	13	12	19	10	62	21	54	13		23
Subtotal TBI	9	35	61	3	58	32	18	35	44	17	111	60	81	13	13	51
TWI																
Western Carolina (WCU)		11	18	31	14	19	6	12	23	6	69	25	33	16	12	24
Charlotte (UNC-C)	1		11	22	33	32	3	1			68	49	56	15	4	50
Subtotal TWI	1	11	29	53	47	51	9	13	23	6	137	74	89	31	16	74
Total Comprehensive	10	46	90	56	105	83	27	48	67	23	248	134	170	44	29	125
Doctoral & Other (6000–13,200)																
TWI only																
Appalachian State (ASU)		7	23	21	22	33	5	9	14	6	50	28	31	17	2	29
Greensboro (UNC-G)	4	3	24	38	27	22	17	20	32	10	91	31	59		13	57
Eastern Carolina (ECU)	3	45	34	31	10	61	12	24	29	8	78	37		58	20	32
State (NCSU)	1	27	28	14	32	6	16	21			90	37	55	3	9	54
Chapel Hill (UNC-CH)			7	63	48	36	3				151	48	98	7	1	78
Total other	8	82	116	167	139	158	53	74	75	24	460	181	243	85	45	250
Grand Total	41	131	280	257	325	299	84	128	155	51	897	477	600	189	109	511

Table B–5
Number of Undergraduate Courses—Humanities

Campus Category & Undergraduate Enrollment	Architecture		Fine Arts			Classical Languages	Romance Languages			German	Russian	Other Foreign Languages	Linguistics	English	Journalism	Speech & Dramatic Arts	Music	Philosophy	Religious Studies, Bible & Religion Education	Arts & Humanities Other
	Architectural Engineering	Architectural Landscaping	Applied	Fine	History & Theory		Spanish	French	Other											
General Baccalaureate (900–3000)																				
TBI																				
Elizabeth City (ECSU)	1		9	6	6		2	2		1			1	21	4	8	23	3		
Winston-Salem (WSSU)			2	4	7		5	6						32	5	11	41	3	8	
Fayetteville (FSU)			10	4	5		11	15		13				35	6	14	35	6	2	4
Subtotal TBI	1		21	14	18		18	23		14			1	88	15	33	99	12	10	4
TWI																				
Asheville (UNC-A)			4	5	5	11	15	15		15			2	20		20	3	22	3	3
Pembroke (PSU)			23	9	12		7	6					4	30	5	22	27	21	32	
Wilmington (UNC-W)			6	9	5	1	22	20	1	5	1	2	4	43	2	28	46	28	15	3
Subtotal TWI			33	23	22	12	44	41	1	20	1	2	10	93	7	70	76	71	50	3
Total General	1		54	37	40	12	62	64	1	34	1	2	11	181	22	103	175	83	60	7

Comprehensive (3400–5700)

TBI

Institution	Values (as printed, left to right)
A and T (NCA & T)	32 16 19 9 7 9 19 6 1 28 19 25 26 5
Central (NCCU)	20 12 8 25 19 20 32 10 26 33 11
Subtotal TBI	32 16 39 21 15 34 38 26 1 60 29 51 59 16

TWI

Institution	Values (as printed, left to right)
Western Carolina (WCU)	4 19 13 17 1 14 14 12 3 1 31 3 35 16 9 8
Charlotte (UNC-C)	14 5 19 6 12 1 16 18 12 1 1 55 16 12 24 40 6
Subtotal TWI	18 5 38 19 29 2 30 32 24 1 4 5 86 3 51 28 33 48 6
Total Comprehensive	50 21 77 40 44 2 64 111 32 2 4 5 146 32 102 87 49 48 6

Doctoral & Other (6000–13,200)

TWI only

Institution	Values (as printed, left to right)
Appalachian State (ASU)	1 26 12 9 10 13 10 7 1 3 39 2 35 45 16 16 2
Greensboro (UNC-G)	1 51 14 25 38 38 41 28 12 1 1 30 3 59 60 37 26 4
Eastern Carolina (ECU)	83 38 23 23 18 18 5 5 78 17 56 55 1 1
State (NCSU)	33 20 16 16 14 4 17 19 10 2 3 2 54 4 26 8 25 14
Chapel Hill (UNC-CH)	7 11 53 44 34 23 37 27 25 35 25 108 31 66 93 54 65 2
Total Other	35 20 183 75 124 96 125 111 90 44 45 31 309 57 242 271 133 121 9
Grand Total	86 41 314 152 208 110 251 286 156 47 51 47 636 111 447 533 265 299 22

Table B-6
Number of Undergraduate Courses—Biological Sciences

Campus Category & Undergraduate Enrollment	Agriculture	Anatomy	Biochemistry	Biology	Biophysics	Botany	Entomology	Forestry	Genetics	Nursing	Pharmacy	Public Health	Medical Technology	Medical Records Technology	Physical & Occupational Therapy	Other	Microbiology	Pharmacology	Physiology	Zoology	Biological Sciences Other
General Baccalaureate (900–3000)																					
TBI																					
Elizabeth City (ECSU)		2	2	4		2	1		2			1					2		3	1	
Winston-Salem (WSSU)		2	1	7		4	1		1	8			1				3	2	4	1	
Fayetteville (FSU)		4		2		1	1		1				7				1		3	3	
Subtotal TBI		8	3	13		7	3		4	8		1	8				6	2	10	5	
TWI																					
Asheville (UNC-A)		1	3	3		2			1								1		1	2	
Pembroke (PSU)		2	3	6		7	1		1								1	2	2	6	
Wilmington (UNC-W)		2	4	14		5			2	4			1				2	1	3	8	
Subtotal TWI		5	10	23		14	1		4	4			1				4	1	6	16	

Comprehensive (3400–5700)																					
TBI																					
A and T (NCA & T)	109	1	3	12		6	2		1	16							4			11	1
Central (NCCU)		5	2	15		5	1		1	20		7				10	2			1	1
Subtotal TBI	109	6	5	27		11	3		2	36		7				10	6			12	2
TWI																					
Western Carolina (WCU)			2	12	1	5		1	2	7	1	5	21	4	1	2	2	2	3	3	
Charlotte (UNC-C)		1	6	10		5			3	7		2		1			6		10	5	1
Subtotal TWI		1	8	22	1	10		1	5	14	1	7	21	5	1	2	8	2	13	8	1
Total Comprehensive	109	7	13	49	1	21	3	1	7	50	1	14	21	5	1	12	14	2	13	20	3
Doctoral & Other (6000–13,200)																					
TWI Only																					
Appalachian State (ASU)			1	8		5	2		1								4	1	1	6	
Greensboro (UNC-G)		2	6	8		6			4	6			4				4	1	5	2	
Eastern Carolina (ECU)		2	4	23	1	6	1		3	31	1	5	13	11	39	32	2		4	3	2
State (NCSU)	80	1	13	5		36	20	32	8			1	1				12		4	22	1
Chapel Hill (UNC-CH)		10	17	4	1	30	1		6			4			1		4	8	11	34	
Total Other	80	15	41	48	1	83	24	32	22	37	1	10	18	11	40	32	26	9	25	67	3
Grand Total	189	35	67	133	2	125	31	33	37	99	2	25	48	16	41	44	50	14	54	108	6

Table B-7
Number of Undergraduate Courses—Physical Sciences

Campus Category & Undergraduate Enrollment	Earth Sciences							Engineering									Math Subjects					
	Astronomy	Chemistry	Computer Science	Geology	Oceanography	Environmental Sciences & Ecology	Other	Aeronautical	Chemical	Civil	Electrical	Engineering Sciences	Mechanical	Nuclear	Industrial Engineering & Technology Arts	Other	Mathematics	Statistics	Meteorology	Physics	Metallurgy	Physical Sciences Other
General Baccalaureate (900–3000)																						
TBI																						
Elizabeth City (ECSU)		9	7	14		10	1								26		11	4		10		
Winston-Salem (WSSU)	1	8	26			3											15	3		6		2
Fayetteville (FSU)		19	14	2													21	2		8		2
Subtotal TBI	1	36	47	16		13	1								26		47	9		24		4
TWI																						
Asheville (UNC-A)		15	8		1	2											16	3	8	14		1
Pembroke (PSU)	1	10	7	4	1	4					2						20	14	1	12		

(UNC-W)	1	15	29	15	3	14	10									21	6	2	21	1
Subtotal TWI	2	40	44	19	5	20	10									57	23	11	47	5
Total General Baccalaureate	3	76	91	35	5	33	11								26	104	32	11	71	
Comprehensive (3400–5700) TBI																				
A and T (NCA & T)	1	38	1			9		13		38		54				48	3		32	
Central (NCCU)	1	20	2	1	1	8		13								24	2		25	
Subtotal TBI	2	58	3	1	1	17		13	13	38		54				72	5		57	
TWI																				
Western Carolina (WCU)	1	22	17	15		10				11		22				23	8	2	15	
Charlotte (UNC-C)	1	17	27	9	2	23	4	34	4	11	1	4	7			35	4	3	15	
Subtotal TWI	1	39	44	24	2	33	4	34	4	11	1	26	7			58	12	5	30	
Total Comprehensive	3	97	47	25	3	50	4	47	4	49	1	80	7			130	17	5	87	
Doctoral & Other (6000–13,200) TWI Only																				
Appalachian State (ASU)	2	14	14	25	1	3		33				24				24	10		20	
Greensboro (UNC-G)	4	22	8			6						36				36	10		23	
Eastern Carolina (ECU)	2	39	16	26	6	3						28				28	4		30	
State (NCSU)	2	38	68	42	7	31	18	42	38	12	29	88	12			48	22	18	21	5
Chapel Hill (UNC-CH)	7	42	29	33	6	23		29		29		39		34	4	34			34	5
Total Other	17	155	135	126	20	66	18	42	38	12	29	121	12			177	80	22	128	5
Grand Total	23	328	273	186	28	149	15									411	129	38	286	5

Table B–8
Percent of Fall 1978 Entering Freshmen Scoring in the 200–499 and 500–800 SAT Score Intervals*

SAT Score Intervals	Doctoral TWI	Non-Doctoral TWI	TBI	All Inst.
Verbal				
500–800	42.8%	17.2%	1.79%	25.3%
200–499	57.2	82.8	98.2	74.6
Math				
500–800	65.7	29.5	2.49	40
200–499	34.3	70.4	97.4	59.9

*Data are taken from the North Carolina Higher Education Data Survey (NCHED) Form A–4. It is not clear whether the School of the Arts is included in these calculations or not. If it is included, it may serve to slightly inflate the non-doctoral TWI distribution, since it has the 4th highest combined SAT mean of all institutions for 1978.

Table B–9
Percent of Fall 1978 Entering Freshmen Scoring in SAT Intervals of 100*[1]

SAT Score Intervals	Doctoral TWI	Non-Doctoral TWI	TBI	All Inst.
Verbal				
700–800	1.1%	0.1%	0.04%	0.5%
600–699	10.1	2.2	0.15	5.1
500–599	31.6	14.9	1.60	19.7
400–499	42.5%	42.3%	9.50%	37.5%
300–399	13.9	35.4	43.90	27.9
200–299	0.8	5.1	44.80	9.2
Math				
700–800	3.7%	0.3%	0.00%	1.6%
600–699	21.0	4.5	0.19	10.5
500–599	41.0	24.7	2.30	27.9
400–499	29.0%	44.8%	13.40%	33.8%
300–399	5.3	23.8	55.30	21.0
200–299	0.0	1.8	28.70	5.1

*North Carolina Higher Education Data Survey (NCHED) Form A–4: First Time Freshman Admission, Fall 1978.

[1]It is not clear whether the School of the Arts is included in these calculations or not. If it is included, it may serve to slightly inflate the non-doctoral PWI distribution, since it has the 4th highest combined SAT mean of all institutions for 1978.

Table B–10
Summary of Mean SAT Scores, 1978 Entering Freshmen

Institutions	Black*			White*			All Students, Combined Score**
	Verbal	Math	Comb.	Verbal	Math	Comb.	
General Baccalaureate							
TBI							
1. Eliz. City	277	306	583	400	368	768	590
2. Winston-Salem	308	333	641	443	422	865	644
3. Fayetteville	268	298	566	336	397	734	588
TWI							
4. Asheville	362	346	708	454	462	916	867
5. Pembroke	327	366	693	390	410	800	813
6. Wilmington	325	347	672	417	445	862	851
Comprehensive							
TBI							
7. A&T	312	341	653	337	382	718	690
8. Central	331	351	682	458	401	859	707
TWI							
9. Western	315	344	659	398	425	823	810
10. Charlotte	389	422	811	444	490	934	927
Doctoral & Other TWI							
11. Appalachian	333	383	716	431	466	897	877
12. Eastern	347	383	730	420	469	879	872
13. Greensboro	385	399	784	471	488	959	952
14. NC State	386	441	828	470	544	1,014	997
15. Chapel Hill	432	448	880	521	564	1,085	1,063
UNC Total	329	356	685	454	495	949	

*Data are taken from UNC Special Survey of Institutions, UNC Planning and Institutional Research, April 1980.
**Computed by the University of North Carlina, Planning Division—General Administration.

Table B–11
Percent of North Carolina Test Takers Applying to UNC, 1978*

VERBAL SAT Score Interval	Blacks	Whites
750–800		95%
700–749	50%	80%
650–699	100%	88%
600–649	69%	87%
550–599	87%	89%
500–549	94%	88%
450–499	92%	89%
400–449	86%	87%
350–399	87%	83%
300–349	86%	79%
250–299	82%	72%
200–249	77%	63%

Table B–12
Percent of Fall 1978 Entering Freshmen Scoring in the 300–499 Interval*

	Doctoral TWI	Non-Doctoral TWI	TBI	All Inst.
Verbal	56.4%	77.7%	53.4%	65.4%
Math	34.3	68.6	68.7	54.8

*Data are taken from the North Carolina Higher Education Data Survey (NCHED) Form A–4. It is not clear whether the School of the Arts is included in these calculations or not. If it is included, it may serve to slightly inflate the non-doctoral TWI distribution, since it has the 4th highest combined SAT mean of all institutions for 1978.

Table B-13
Actual Number of 1979 Entering Freshman Scoring in the Low SAT Ranges*

SCORE INTERVALS:	VERBAL			MATH		
	200–299	300–399	200–399	200–299	300–399	200–399
TBIs						
Eliz. City	213	74	287	141	134	275
Winston-Salem	239	224	463	144	296	440
Fayetteville	213	100	313	159	144	303
A&T	372	376	748	189	450	639
Central	146	303	449	90	329	419
TOTALS	1,183	1,077	2,260	723	1,353	2,076
Non-Doctoral TWIs						
Asheville	4	44	48	4	43	47
Pembroke	10	146	156	1	123	124
Wilmington	47	361	408	24	228	252
Western	109	617	726	64	470	534
Charlotte	15	354	369	5	148	153
Appalachian	63	671	734	22	351	373
Eastern	133	873	1,066	26	481	507
TOTALS	381	3,066	3,447	146	1,844	1,990
Doctoral & Other TWIs						
Chapel Hill	26	330	356	4	164	168
NCSU	46	518	564	8	121	129
Greensboro	1	201	202	0	92	92
TOTALS	73	1,049	1,122	12	377	389

*Data taken from Statistical Abstract of Higher Education in North Carolina, 1979–1980, Table 63.

APPENDIX C

Financial Data

Table C-1
Current Operating Expenditures Per FTE Student by Institutional Group and Expenditure Category in Constant (1977) Dollars, for Selected Time Periods 1964–1978

Institutional Group	Expenditure Category[1]	1964–66	1970–72	1976–78
General Baccalaureate TBIs	Net Operating Expense	2,164	2,802	2,794
ECSU	Academic	1,057	1,693	1,487
FSU	Support	217	491	476
WSSU	Physical Plant	297	502	491
	Other	593	116	340
General Baccalaureate TWIs	Net Operating Expense	1,670	2,569	2,601
UNC-W	Academic	1,144	1,468	1,543
PSU	Support	250	392	396
UNC-A	Physical Plant	174	366	397
	Other	102	343	265
Comprehensive TBIs	Net Operating Expense	2,466	2,667	2,688
NCA&T	Academic	1,293	1,662	1,618
	Support	223	378	374
NCCU	Physical Plant	337	438	513
	Other	613	189	183
Comprehensive TWIs	Net Operating Expense	2,127	2,537	2,601
UNC-C	Academic	1,244	1,741	1,762
	Support	206	303	311
WCU	Physical Plant	238	327	379
	Other	439	166	149
Small Other TWIs	Net Operating Expense	1,873	2,486	2,828
ASU	Academic	1,139	1,418	1,656
ECU	Support	179	302	325
UNC-G	Physical Plant	239	342	393
	Other	316	424	454

	Large Other TWIs	UNC-CH	NCSU
Net Operating Expense	3,246	4,175	4,285
Academic	2,358	2,905	2,925
Support	239	476	479
Physical Plant	363	504	637
Other	286	290	244

[1]Categories are defined as follows:

Net Operating Expense = Current Operating Expenditures − Student Aid*

Academic = Instruction and Departmental Research + Other Research + Library

Support = Administration + Student Services + Data Processing

Physical Plant = Plant Maintenance

Other = Summer School, Extension, Debt Service and Miscellaneous.

(*Includes only that portion of student aid budgeted as an expenditure)

Table C–2
Percentage Distribution of Net Operating Expenditures and Its Components by Institutional Group and Time Period

Institutional Group	Expenditure Category[1]	1964–66	1970–72	1976–78
General Baccalaureate TBIs	Net Operating Expense	5.5	4.5	4.9
ECSU	Academic	4.1%	4.2%	4.2%
FSU	Support	6.5	6.4	7.0
WSSU	Physical Plant	6.4	6.1	5.8
	Other	10.6	2.2	6.9
General Baccaulaureate TWIs	Net Operating Expense	3.3	4.7	5.2
UNC-W	Academic	3.5%	4.1%	4.8%
PSU	Support	5.8	5.8	6.5
UNC-A	Physical Plant	2.9	5.0	5.2
	Other	1.4	6.6	6.0
Comprehensive TBIs	Net Operating Expense	10.8	8.3	8.0
NCA&T	Academic	8.6%	7.9%	7.6%
	Support	11.4	9.5	9.3
NCCU	Physical Plant	12.4	10.2	10.2
	Other	18.8	6.2	6.2
Comprehensive TWIs	Net Operating Expense	6.1	8.5	10.0
UNC-C	Academic	5.5%	9.0%	10.6%
	Support	6.9	8.3	9.9
WCU	Physical Plant	5.7	8.3	9.6
	Other	11.3	5.9	5.8
Small Other TWIs	Net Operating Expense	21.5	22.9	24.3
ASU	Academic	19.9%	20.1%	22.3%
ECU	Support	24.0	22.6	23.2
UNC-G	Physical Plant	23.0	23.7	22.4
	Other	25.4	41.4	44.3
Large Other TWIs	Net Operating Expense	52.8	51.1	47.6
UNC-CH	Academic	58.4%	54.7%	50.7%
	Support	48.4	47.4	44.1
NCSU	Physical Plant	49.5	46.7	46.8
	Other	32.5	37.7	30.7

Table C–3
Components of Net Operating Expenditures As a Percentage of Total by Institutional Group and Time Period

Institutional Group	Expenditure Category[1]	1964-66	1970-72	1976-78
General Baccalaureate TBIs	Net Operating Expense	100.0	100.0	100.0
ECSU	Academic	48.8%	60.4%	53.2%
FSU	Support	10.0	17.5	17.0
WSSU	Physical Plant	13.7	17.9	17.6
	Other	27.5	4.2	12.2
General Baccalaureate TWIs	Net Operating Expense	100.0	100.0	100.0
UNC-W	Academic	68.5%	57.1%	59.3%
PSU	Support	15.0	15.3	15.2
UNC-A	Physical Plant	10.4	14.2	15.3
	Other	6.1	13.2	10.2
Comprehensive TBIs	Net Operating Expense	100.0	100.0	100.0
NCA&T	Academic	52.4%	62.3%	60.2%
	Support	9.0	14.2	13.9
NCCU	Physical Plant	13.7	16.4	19.1
	Other	24.9	7.1	6.8
Comprehensive TWIs	Net Operating Expense	100.0	100.0	100.0
UNC-C	Academic	58.5%	68.6%	67.7%
	Support	9.7	11.9	12.0
WCU	Physical Plant	11.2	12.9	14.6
	Other	20.6	6.6	5.7
Small Other TWIs	Net Operating Expense	100.0	100.0	100.0
ASU	Academic	60.8%	57.0%	58.6%
ECU	Support	9.6	12.1	11.5
UNC-G	Physical Plant	12.8	13.8	13.9
	Other	16.9	17.1	16.0
Large Other TWIs	Net Operating Expense	100.0	100.0	100.0
UNC-CH	Academic	72.6%	69.6%	68.3%
	Support	7.4	11.4	11.2
NCSU	Physical Plant	11.2	12.1	14.9
	Other	8.8	6.9	5.6

[1]For definitions, see Table F–1.

Table C-4

Measures of Capital Stock and Capital Expenditures Per FTE Student by Institutional Group, for Selected Time Periods 1964–1978

Institutional Group	Measure of Capital Stock/Expenditure		1964-66	1970-72	1976-78
General Baccalaureate TBIs	Replacement Value of Property / Capital Appropriation	Constant (1977) $s	8,867 / 3,736	12,883 / 2,390	9,466 / 707
ECSU FSU WSSU	Book Value of Plant Assets / Additions to Plant	Current Dollars	3,597 / 449	7,619 / 297	8,284 / 917
General Baccalaureate TWIs	Replacement Value of Property / Capital Appropriation	Constant (1977) $s	5,176 / 3,627	8,268 / 1,915	8,403 / 574
UNC-W PSU UNC-A	Book Value of Plant Assets / Additions to Plant	Current Dollars	2,394 / 579	5,560 / 1,020	7,181 / 813
Comprehensive TBIs	Replacement Value of Property / Capital Appropriation	Constant (1977) $s	9,690 / 2,798	10,515 / 1,668	8,798 / 223
NCA&T NCCU	Book Value of Plant Assets / Additions to Plant	Current Dollars	4,582 / 514	5,996 / 242	7,103 / 411
Comprehensive TWIs	Replacement Value of Property / Capital Appropriation	Constant (1977) $s	9,773 / 4,050	9,565 / 2,201	8,489 / 410
UNC-C WCU	Book Value of Plant Assets / Additions to Plant	Current Dollars	5,262 / 1,119	6,318 / 833	7,177 / 572
Small Other TWIs	Replacement Value of Property / Capital Appropriation	Constant (1977) $s	11,956 / 3,252	11,654 / 1,252	10,594 / 367
ASU ECU UNC-G	Book Value of Plant Assets / Additions to Plant	Current Dollars	4,318 / 679	5,845 / 480	7,776 / 791
Large Other TWIs	Replacement Value of Property / Capital Appropriation	Constant (1977) $s	17,427 / 3,736	17,495 / 1,158	14,642 / 232
UNC-CH NCSU	Book Value of Plant Assets / Additions to Plant	Current Dollars	3,597 / 449	10,318 / 743	10,757 / 596

Table C–5
Percentage Distribution of Capital Stock and Capital Expenditures by Institutional Group and Time Period

Institutional Group	Measure of Capital Stock/Expenditure	1964–66	1970–72	1976–78
General Baccalaureate TBIs	Replacement Value of Property Capital Appropriation	4.3% 8.2	4.9% 8.1	4.8% 12.4
ECSU FSU WSSU	Book Value of Plant Assets Additions to Plant	3.7 4.0	5.0 1.8	5.4 8.0
General Baccalaureate TWIs	Replacement Value of Property Capital Appropriation	2.0% 4.0	3.6% 10.9	4.6% 10.4
UNC-W PSU UNC-A	Book Value of Plant Assets Additions to Plant	2.1 4.3	4.2 9.7	5.4 8.0
Comprehensive TBIs	Replacement Value of Property Capital Appropriation	8.2% 9.6	7.8% 10.9	7.6% 6.5
NCA&T NCCU	Book Value of Plant Assets Additions to Plant	8.4 8.2	7.7 3.9	7.9 7.7
Comprehensive TWIs	Replacement Value of Property Capital Appropriation	5.4% 9.3	7.6% 15.7	9.3% 15.1
UNC-C WCU	Book Value of Plant Assets Additions to Plant	6.6 12.2	8.4 14.6	10.6 10.7
Small Other TWIs	Replacement Value of Property Capital Appropriation	26.1% 29.3	25.4 24.4	26.5% 30.5
ASU ECU UNC-G	Book Value of Plant Assets Additions to Plant	22.4 30.5	22.4 22.9	25.3 33.3
Large Other TWIs	Replacement Value of Property Capital Appropriation	54.0% 39.6	50.7% 30.0	47.2% 25.1
UNC-CH NCSU	Book Value of Plant Assets Additions to Plant	56.8 40.8	52.3 47.1	45.4 32.3

Table C–6
Distribution of FTE Faculty Members and Annual Library Book Acquisitions by Institutional Group, for Selected Time Periods 1964–1978

Institutional Group	Resource	1964–66	1970–72	1976–78
General Baccalaureate TBIs				
ECSU FSU WSSU	Student-Faculty Ratio	14.6	14.0	16.8
	Library Books Acquired Per FTE Student	2.7	2.5	2.4
General Baccalaureate TWIs				
UNC-W PSU UNC-A	Student-Faculty Ratio	15.6	15.5	16.0
	Library Books Acquired Per FTE Student	5.3	4.1	5.4
Comprehensive TBIs				
NCA&T NCCU	Student-Faculty Ratio	15.2	15.2	16.1
	Library Books Acquired Per FTE Student	2.8	2.8	2.7
Comprehensive TWIs				
UNC-C WCU	Student-Faculty Ratio	17.8	15.4	16.0
	Library Books Acquired Per FTE Student	5.6	4.1	3.8
Small Other TWIs				
ASU ECU UNC-G	Student-Faculty Ratio	18.4	15.2	16.0
	Library Books Acquired Per FTE Student	2.9	3.1	3.1
Large Other TWIs				
UNC-CH NCSU	Student-Faculty Ratio	13.2	13.0	13.3
	Library Books Acquired Per FTE Student	4.0	3.7	4.0

Table C–7
Distribution of Total FTE Students by Institutional Group and Time Period

Institutional Group	Enrollment Measure	1964–66	1970–72	1976–78
General Baccalaureate TBIs	Number of FTE Students[1]	3,180	3,650	5,470
ECSU FSU WSSU	Percent of UNC Total	6.5	5.1	5.7
General Baccalaureate TWIs	Number of FTE Students[1]	2,467	4,143	6,101
UNC-W PSU UNC-A	Percent of UNC Total	5.0	5.8	6.6
Comprehensive TBIs	Number of FTE Students[1]	5,448	7,025	9,142
NCA&T NCCU	Percent of UNC Total	11.1	10.0	9.9
Comprehensive TWIs	Number of FTE Students[1]	3,576	7,626	11,727
UNC-C WCU	Percent of UNC Total	7.3	10.7	12.7
Small Other TWIs	Number of FTE Students[1]	14,272	20,851	26,312
ASU ECU UNC-G	Percent of UNC Total	29.0	29.3	28.5
Large Other TWIs	Number of FTE Students[1]	20,209	27,754	33,934
UNC-CH NCSU	Percent of UNC Total	41.1	39.6	36.6

[1]Annual average for the two years.

Table C–8
Alternative Measures of Capital Stock Per Pupil by Institutional Group, for 1978

Institutional Group	Pupil Measures	Gross Square Feet	Capital Stock Measures	
			N.A. Non-Residential[1]	N.A. Instructional[2]
General Baccalaureate TBIs				
ECSU	Per Enrolled Student	280	135	61
FSU	Per FTE	297	143	65
WSSU	Per Credit Hour	16.8	8.1	3.7
General Baccalaureate TWIs				
UNC-W	Per Enrolled Student	204	110	77
PSU	Per FTE	253	136	95
UNC-A	Per Credit Hour	16.8	9.0	6.3
Comprehensive TBIs				
NCA&T	Per Enrolled Student	270	134	42
	Per FTE	292	145	45
NCCU	Per Credit Hour	16.8	8.3	2.6
Comprehensive TWIs				
UNC-C	Per Enrolled Student	208	87	58
	Per FTE	260	109	72
WCU	Per Credit Hour	15.6	6.6	4.6
Small Other TWIs				
ASU	Per Enrolled Student	232	104	62
ECU	Per FTE	272	122	72
UNC-G	Per Credit Hour	17.3	7.8	4.8
Large Other TWIs				
UNC-CH	Per Enrolled Student	360	N/A	N/A
	Per FTE	410	N/A	N/A
NCSU	Per Credit Hour	27.5	N/A	N/A

[1]Net-Assignable Non-Residential Square Feet
[2]Net-Assignable Instructional Square Feet in Satisfactory Condition

Table C–9
Relationship Between Total Enrollment, FTE Students and Student Credit Hours by Institutional Group, for Selected Years 1970–1978

Institutional Group	Relationships	1970	1972	1976	1978
General Baccalaureate TBIs					
ECSU FSU WSSU	Total Students Divided by FTE	1.15	1.15	1.05	1.06
	FTE Divided by Student Credit Hour	17.6	18.2	17.3	17.7
General Baccalaureate TWIs					
UNC-W PSU UNC-A	Total Students Divided by FTE	1.26	1.14	1.22	1.24
	FTE Divided by Student Credit Hour	13.7	15.8	16.4	15.1
Comprehensive TBIs					
NCA&T NCCU	Total Students Divided by FTE	1.12	1.14	1.13	1.08
	FTE Divided by Student Credit Hour	17.0	17.0	16.8	17.4
Comprehensive TWIs					
UNC-C WCU	Total Students Divided by FTE	1.41	1.24	1.23	1.25
	FTE Divided by Student Credit Hour	14.4	15.8	16.5	16.7
Small Other TWIs					
ASU ECU UNC-G	Total Students Divided by FTE	1.18	1.15	1.15	1.17
	FTE Divided by Student Credit Hour	N/A	15.7	15.9	15.7
Large Other TWIs					
UNC-CH NCSU	Total Students Divided by FTE	1.20	1.12	1.12	1.14
	FTE Divided by Student Credit Hour	14.5	N/A	14.7	14.9

Index